Marilyn,
know that ____
Loves ye
desires ____
for your ____
Carla!

Beloved

Experiencing God as Abba in a Fatherless Generation

Carla R. Cannon

CANNON**PUBLISHING**

Beloved

Experiencing God as Abba in a Fatherless Generation

Carla R. Cannon

CANNONPUBLISHING

Cannon Publishing

P.O. Box 1298

Greenville, NC 27835

Phone: 888-502-2228

Website: www.cannonpublishing.net

Printed in the United States of America, North Carolina.

Printed in the United States of America.

ISBN: 9781090400611

If you desire to order copies in bulk, please contact Carla R. Cannon Enterprises at 888-502-2228 Extension 2.

"*Beloved,* I pray that all may go well with you and that you may be in good health, as it goes well with your soul."

- 3 John 1:2 (ESV)

Contents

Chapter Ten

Dedication

I dedicate this book to anyone who has suffered from rejection and abandonment. Know that you are not alone, and God accepts you just as you are.

There is purpose hidden in all that you have had to endure.

It is my prayer that you will find healing in my story. I share with an intention to let you know that you are not alone. Daddy (and Mommy) issues are more prevalent than ever before and although we can't rewrite our history, we control our destiny.

Use what you've been through to help someone else overcome. Share your story. Write the book! Release the blog! Launch the nonprofit! Do it!

Let others know they are not bound by what happened to them because in due time, God is going to Romans 8:28 all you've ever encountered.

Remember, no longer do you have to feel ashamed of where you come from, it helped shape you into the person you are today, and you my friend are God's dearly ***Beloved!***

BELOVED

Be • Lov • ed

adjective

1.   Dearly loved.

Synonyms: *darling, dear, dearest, precious, adored, loved, much loved, favored.*

noun

2.   A much-loved person.

Synonyms: *sweetheart, loved one, love, true love, dear one, lover."*

Introduction

Why I Decided to Write This Book Now

Now more than ever I am witnessing more people being affected by what we have come to know as "Daddy Issues." Growing up with my father being inconsistent in my life was one of the most painful experiences I've ever encountered.

I've always found it selfish for people to shout, "Get over it!" to someone who is expressing hurt regarding something they have experienced personally that has affected them in a negative way. I really don't think it matters if it was a year ago or ten years ago; pain is pain.

However, society teaches us to K.I.M.; Keep it moving! Guess what? I did that for years which led to a sudden crash when I realized I could no longer ignore the pain I felt but in order to heal it, I had to reveal it. That meant facing it.

Truth is, we all want to be healed, feel loved and lead successful lives however, it's the process that we have trouble contending with. Confronting our pain as well as our abusers (or even those who have neglected us) can be a scary thing.

It wasn't until I was in my twenties when I finally asked my Dad the question, "Why did you leave me?" His reply pierced my soul and immediately the anger I felt toward him shifted to sadness. He said, "I didn't leave you. You were taken away from me." As tears filled my eyes, He continued to say, "Baby, you used to live with me before your Mom took you from me."

I'm sure you could imagine that by now I was balling with tears streaming down my face with my anger suddenly shifting to my mother. The interesting thing about anger is it doesn't care who it is mad it, it just needs something or someone to blame. At this time, that person was no longer my Dad; it was my Mom who would soon feel my wrath.

It is stories like these where you will hear more of that I've never shared in any of my books until now. Why? Because you want to protect those you love. I never wanted anyone to dislike my parents or think I was harsh for sharing my truth.

However, as an entrepreneur I encounter many women as clients who suffer from abandonment and rejection issues that originate from absent fathers (and sometimes mothers) and I felt it was time to address the elephant in the room.

Pain can make you do some interesting things and not at all am I blaming those who have hurt me, but I am sharing how I chose to respond to it at one point in my life.

Inside **BELOVED** I am bearing my soul and for the first time I am going deeper into my story and unveil the hidden issues I once had that led to my addiction to alcohol, marijuana, pornography and sex.

Uncovering one's self is never comfortable or easy. But I believe people have heard and read enough junk that it's time for true intervention. So many are tired of acting out due to traumatic experiences and they want to overcome, but it's challenging to find real people who will pause from trying to be perfect on social media and unveil their scars to heal a hurting generation.

"They have conquered him by the blood of the lamb, and by the word of their testimony." - Revelation 12:11

It is my heart's desire that this book will start a conversation that is long overdue with our parents and loved ones. Daughters need their fathers. Sons need their fathers. Daughters need their mothers. Sons need their mothers. PERIOD!

Family secrets are killing the spirit of many people and it's time to peel the carpet back and sweep out all the junk we have kept hidden for so long.

Within the pages of this book I will also be tackling the issues of healing from spiritual parent wounds as I have had my share of this as well. I take you on a journey of how my unrealistic expectations led me down a path to be manipulated (at times) and disappointed because I continued to look for people to do what only God can do.

Remember: You are God's *BELOVED* and your entire life is a love story written about you coming to know Him. God is whatever we need Him to be, whenever we need him to be it.

In order to heal the ache within the depths of my soul, I had to learn to accept Abba (Father) as the Dad I have been searching for much of my life. Learning to let go of all the hurt, pain and unanswered questions has been a vital part of my journey to healing and experiencing wholeness.

> *"Even if my father and mother abandon*
> *me, the LORD will hold me close."*
> *- Psalm 27:10 (NLT)*

If you will allow me, I'd like to join you on your journey to healing as well. You don't have to remain hurt and scarred from traumatic encounters. Healing and love are available to you.

Let's face this mountain of a mess together and bring it tumbling down by facing these giants head on!

Oh yeah, and don't be alarmed if you find yourself shedding tears as you read my story. Trust me, I was probably crying as I typed it. It takes a lot of courage to revisit some of the most painful points of your life, let alone express it to the world.

People can be very judgmental and critical but guess what? They weren't there! I was. Same as it relates to your story. You no longer need to apologize for the anger or frustrations you feel but you can finally let it out as we journey through together.

I do ask that as you read along, and something resonates with you, let me know. I'd love to hear about it as it serves as tremendous encouragement to know that your story has helped even one person.

My email is: **Carla@womenofstandard.org** and yes, I check it myself LOL Are you ready? Let's do this!

A Letter to Daughters Who Feel Fatherless

All my life I wanted nothing more than to be Daddy's Little Girl. I wanted this so badly that I once bought a necklace for myself with a pendant that read these exact words and wore it every day.

Did it fill any void? No, but it brought about comfort wearing it. It gave me a sense of belonging even if only temporarily.

I felt that if someone noticed it, the word "orphan" would be erased that had been engraved on my forehead for all to see.

One thing I won't do is lie and tell you that reading this book will mend the brokenness you feel deep down within your soul. But what I can promise is that you'll receive insight, strength, courage and a sense of not being alone in all you've had to carry.

In reading **BELOVED**, you will learn the significance and value that Christ brings to your life. He's there, fully aware and ready to wrap you in His arms and melt all the pain away.

I've experienced enough pain for hundreds of women, perhaps that is why people flock to me and find it so easy to share their inner most secrets. It's always amazing to know there are other people in the world who have overcome the very thing you may currently be struggling with. That's the great thing about life; we are all on our own unique journey.

It is my hope through sharing another segment of my story that you will learn to gravitate to God and not people. A substitute is okay, but remember, there's nothing like the real thing *baby*.

People will disappoint, but God will never fail you. It is my hope that you and I will journey together into our season of healing, forgiving ourselves (and others) to a path of purpose and total recovery.

I've been helping people a long time almost at the expense of my own health and sanity. One valuable thing I finally learned was how to pause, pull back and take the same principles I was sharing with others and use it to help myself. People are selfish by nature and if you let them, they will take all you have to give; leaving you with nothing.

I invite you while on this journey to pay attention to the emotions you feel as you read my story and develop the courage to one day share your own from a place of power rather than pain and pity.

Please note, I love both of my parents and all we have encountered together has made me the woman I am today. It wasn't until I became a parent myself that I learned how tough raising a child really was. Now, I apply more grace coupled with understanding. But growing up I was angry and often left confused as to why I had to be the child no one wanted (or at least that's how I felt).

I am tearing up as I write this because sometimes even with my success, I still feel like an orphan. Struggling to find the right church home; the right spiritual leaders who can nurture the gifts God has placed on the inside of me.

At times, I feel stuck and as if I've done all I can do with my business in which I share both my natural and supernatural gifts with the world. Feeling weak and fatigued, I enter into my prayer closet, and come back out refreshed and recharged, ready to take on the world!

I am sharing this because so many see my outward success (and I haven't even scratched the surface of all God wants to do in my life) and think I have it going on. My life isn't all peaches and cream; TRUST ME.

Some days I wake up depressed, sad and alone. Wondering, is what I'm doing really helping anyone? Do people really love me? Or do they like what I've accomplished and what I can in turn do for them? If they knew my frailties would they still rush to snap a selfie with me, or share my posts on social media?

Other days I feel happy, alive and loved. That's life for ya, huh?

Despite it all, what keeps me sane and moving forward is my relationship with Christ.

At the point of writing this book, I don't speak to many people in my family. Each time I would be around them I felt like the outsider; the "pretend" cousin, rather than a daughter, or niece.

I grew tired of all the lies and gossip. Nothing could be shared with one person without them running and telling the other and then the other one tells another. Is anything sacred anymore?

Does this sound like your family? Then, great! That means we all have issues and I don't have to worry about you judging my truth. I grew tired of living a lie and posting selfies as if everything was all good when it wasn't. I've pulled back a bit from social media because honestly, I was becoming overwhelmed by it all. Some things I wish we could go back to from the good ole days. Such as beepers and pagers. LOL Do you remember when you had to wait until someone called you back?

Now, folks can text or call your phone and if that fails, they can message you on social media, send an audio message or even call you from it or some random app. It's all too much.

I am that girl who went on social media and blocked most of my family. Sounds rude right? Well, as my favorite comedian Kevin Hart would say, *Let Me Explain...*

I only did it because one day I was crying out to my Mom about how I never hear from her and so forth and she had the nerve to say, "Well, your whole life is on social media so when I want to know what's going on with you, I just go there."

Thinking, I would fix her (shout out to Iyanla-ha!), I went on a tangent and blocked everyone in our family, even some of her friends that I knew she spoke to often. This act was nothing toward them, but it was more so to deny her access to me to the point, she would have to pick up the phone and call to see how I was doing. Or at least, not be too busy to chat with me for a second when I called her.

Can you say, Epic Fail? It was exactly that. She didn't call or text any more, or less. Come to think of it, they are still blocked now. Even her! OOPS!

It is my prayer that God will mend my relationship with my family, but truth is, sometimes he doesn't. Sometimes people can't see past mistakes you've made and will never be in your corner cheering you on.

You know what? We simply must accept it. Some things are the way they are. I have one sister who is four years older than me and I've spent over thirty years trying to figure out why she pulls away from me rather than gravitate toward me.

Here I am the girl who is all about authentic sisterhood, yet her own sister wants nothing to do with her. How embarrassing. I almost gave it all up and went and got a normal 9 to 5. Seriously.

Then I suddenly came to my senses and said, oh no, I will not allow pain to dictate my life. I will feel it and not only function, but WIN! I will face it and although I can't erase it, no longer shall it control me.

I grew extremely tired of anyone I would talk to telling me to pray and how God would fix it. Sometimes, you just want to slap them or bite their ear off like Tyson just so they can get a feel of what you experience in your throbbing soul every day.

I know it's the right thing to say when someone is estranged from their family. I've heard every kind of prophesy there is about "God said" this, and "God said" that. At this point, I had to protect my sanity and remove myself.

I still talk to my Mom here and there, but our relationship is nothing like it was; not at the time of writing this book. You may be reading this in March (the release date); so, let's pray that it's shifted by then.

As far as my Dad, we've recently connected (again). Let's pray we remain in each other's life this time around.

But if not, I'm learning to be content with my beautiful daughter, Patience. Sometimes, I fear she will grow older and forget all about me. I've heard horrible stories about daughters going to college and literally losing their minds. Please pray for Patience and that we remain close. Like seriously, I need you to pray!

As she approaches her senior year in high school, I admit I get a bit of anxiety. It's real scary to know that your child will soon enter this cold world they so anxiously desire. Not knowing the hearts of so many have waxed cold.

I took a moment to write this to you to provide hope despite what you may be facing. Life isn't all bad. Despite my humorous yet painful stories, I have great people in my life. Truth is, no matter how awesome they are, none of them can replace the relationship with my mom, my dad and my sister.

So, you know what? I simply stopped trying. I had to learn how to embrace new people for who they are and not try to turn them into a "sister" if they are not that. Having friends makes life so much more enjoyable and honestly, they become like family.

But one of the worst things I could have ever done was try to replace my Mom and Dad just because someone else embraced me. People always had a way of reminding you that you weren't really family. This includes calling spiritual leaders my Dad or Mom as well. But hey, we all must learn huh? Life tends to know just how to teach us.

Blood isn't always thicker than water. The only blood we should focus on is the blood Jesus shed on Calvary.

But I admit, I struggled in relationships with friends because my relationships with my family were always dysfunctional and no one ever really taught me how to be a friend.

We all know the two sisters who haven't spoken in years for whatever silly reason, or the cousins who tend to fight every time there's a family function. But it all becomes the norm. There's no Big Mama around to say, 'Enough! This is not what family does!'

I always hated the family sayings, 'We all we got!" or "Family over Everything!" or "Blood is thicker than water." They always made me mad and I begged to differ because that wasn't my reality.

Now do I still yearn for a relationship with my Dad? Sure. Would I like a closer relationship with my Mom? Absolutely. But after writing our book, *Redeeming the Time* in May 2018, issues came to the surface that she simply was not ready to deal with.

I ended up pulling that book off the shelf and felt like such a failure. During the time of writing it, my Mom and I were growing closer (and so was my sister and I; or so I thought.) But something happened at the book signing that took me all the way back to my childhood.

The pain, agony, defeat and embarrassment I felt while sitting there in front of a room full of people when my mom downplayed the level of trauma her ex-husband took *all of us* through growing up was indescribable.

Then, she allowed her friend to host the event whose mother passed many years ago and they were very close. Her friend went on to say for most of the event how women need to reach out to their mothers, and how God only gives you one and blah blah blah.

As I sat there, I thought of the women who were in the room, whose stories I knew. One was molested by her mother, another was abandoned by hers and the stories went on.

I just want parents to take responsibility for their stuff sometimes. You know? As a mother now, I am careful to ensure Patience has a voice in our home. Mine was taken as a child. Everyone told me I talked too much and that's how I learned to talk fast so I could get it out quickly without anyone interrupting me.

This book I must admit is costing me the most, because many of these issues are still pending. But hey, it's my reality. Society today may refer to my writings as "spilling the tea," but that's not my intention.

This is more about me than it is those who have hurt me because although I share the pain, I also include how it launched me into my life purpose!

It's easy to write about what God has brought you out of, but what about the things He prompts you to share that you are standing in right now?

The things you prefer to keep to yourself. The things that in most families they would dare you to tell. Instead you just sweep it under the rug and pretend it never happened.

I've seen so much of that. I am tired of innocent daughters growing up thinking one man is *Daddy* when their real *Daddy* lives up the street. Or daughters being molested by people who should be protecting them, and mothers not believing them or have the audacity to remain with their child's abuser out of fear or whatever absurd excuse they come up with.

The interesting thing is, it wasn't until the other day when I was having a conversation with a friend of mine that I realized my older cousin had molested me when I was younger. I always called it fondling because there was no penetration involved. But on this journey, I've learned in order to heal it, you must first acknowledge it for what it *really* is. So yes, my older cousin molested me and to this day I never told anyone other than my friend I was talking to that day...and now you.

It's all sick and we must begin sharing our stories. What's the worst that can happen? No one can tell your story like you! When they try to use it against you, like they did when I wrote my first book, The Power in Waiting, tell them: "I wrote a book about that boo and it's an international best-seller! Check your local book store or grab it from Amazon rather than receive second hand information!" (Drops mic and exits stage left)

Chapter One

Growing Up

On June 22, 1984 I was born to Roscoe and Felicia Cannon in Heidelburg, Germany. My father was in the military and they were totally not expecting me.

I remember how I used to enjoy hearing my mom tell me the story of how everyone expected a boy and I popped out a girl. They had no name for me therefore, my Mom said the nurse named me Carla "R" that stood for "Right on Little Roscoe."

I was told I came out looking just like my Dad. I don't remember much about my mom and dad being together except for what she would tell me growing up.

What I do remember is that I hated not having a middle name. It seemed like everyone had one. But I was stuck with "R." Instead of seeing the significance of my name I began to despise it.

I know what I'll do, I'll give myself a middle name. Rachel! I'd declare. No, that's my paternal Grandmother's name. Renee! Hmmm no. I got it! Rochelle! That was it! I was now Carla Rochelle Cannon.

I never went through any formal name change or anything but as I grew older, I used that name on everything. I signed my permit and license: Carla R. Cannon. The only two places you did not find "Rochelle" was on my social security card and birth certificate.

Growing up with my Dad I do remember him dancing and singing all the time. He would turn the radio on and dance with me while singing and laughing all hard. I would have a blast with him. I was totally a Daddy's girl. There was no other place I wanted to be than with my Dad. It didn't matter how much money he had or where he lived. All that mattered was that I was with him, and we were together.

It all becomes a blur from us living in Germany to my mom being married to her second husband which became my stepdad. That's where a lot of the pain came from that I can remember.

I've also learned that I am horrible with dates, so I don't even recall how old I was, only how I felt during those moments.

I think I did know or learn that my Dad struggled with alcohol addiction and was discharged from the Army because of it. I remember him being in prison and while there my Grandmother Rachel died. Now, here I think I was about 11 or 12 years old (don't ask how I remember that; I could be wrong LOL). I don't recall if my Dad was able to come home for my

Grandmother's funeral or not. But I believe that's when his life took an even darker turn, when he lost his mom.

Grandma Rachel was everybody's favorite. Her and my Grandfather Ray (who has now also passed away) were Jehovah's Witnesses therefore, my Dad grew up eating turkey whenever and not receiving Christmas gifts.

I remember telling my Grandfather Ray one time, "Granddaddy, it's Thanksgiving, we are supposed to be eating turkey." He'd turn to me with a stern look and say, "I can eat turkey anytime." I don't recall really having a relationship with my granddaddy. I do remember as a kid growing up looking at his white, ashy feet wishing he would put some lotion on them. I think I even volunteered before. That was the first and last. LOL

But my Grandmother was a sweetheart. I would go door to door with her and vaguely remember her telling strangers about Jehovah. The funny thing is I don't recall anyone being rude to my Grandmother. I mean how could you, she was super sweet and extremely loving. She was the type, that even if you didn't agree with her faith, you'd still welcome her inside and offer her tea just to be in her presence.

I remember going to the Kingdom Hall with her and one of her favorite songs was "Life Without End at Last." When she died, I asked my Grandfather if I could have her bible and psalm book. I kept them both for a long time. I couldn't recall the tune in which Grandma Rachel's favorite song was supposed to be sung so whenever I was sad, I'd open it and sing it in whatever tune came to mind.

After rehearsing it a few times, I had created my own rhythm and even learned the words by heart. Let's see what I remember: *"Can you see, with your brown eyes, people all living together.... Sorrow has passed, peace at last.... Life without tears and pain... Sing out with joy of heart, you too can have a part. Live for the day, when you'll say, life without end at last."*

It's amazing the things we remember as kids huh? I ended up losing those books in a flood one year in North Carolina where I lived and boy, did I cry.

As a way of keeping in touch with her, I would write Grandma Rachel letters all the time telling her how much I missed her. Even when I became a mother, I always wondered what life would be like if she were here and what type of relationship she and Patience would have.

By the age of twelve (or so) I now had no living grandmother on either side of my family. My maternal grandmother, Lillie Coward, I don't remember anything about her; I was about two years old when she passed away. However, I do remember my mom telling me how my Grandmother was trying to help potty train me, but I would always pee on the bed. She said, "The day after my mama died, you never peed on the bed again." How ironic is that?

EXPERIENCING CHILD ABUSE

My mom had divorced my dad and I am not sure how much time had passed, but eventually she remarried. At first, I liked him, but my mom always told me I liked the wrong guys she dated. She said, the nice ones I paid no mind but clung to the no-good ones.

I remember when people used to think I was his daughter and it felt great because I wasn't seeing my dad too much around this time. It was unclear as of why. I just knew he wasn't around, and I grew accustomed to not seeing him. I called him Dad.

Every morning in the winter time my sister and I would wake up to a glass of Alka-Seltzer waiting for us to drink to prevent us from catching a cold. It was disgusting. I would gag everytime and literally had to force it down. But I guess it worked, because we never got sick.

I grew up in an environment where I'd hear my mom and my stepdad arguing and fighting and it was always over money. One time, the front door swung open and my mom went running down the street to our neighbor's house with her purse. I remember our neighbor, Ms. Belinda dared him to come into her house. He never did. It's funny how even abusive men know their limits.

It was very embarrassing because Ms. Belinda had kids: Samantha, Anita (we called her Punkin), and Victoria. We all went to school together. Samantha and my sister were close and Punkin and I were hmmm friends, I guess. I used to go over to their house often and eat up their oodles and noodles. I think we simply tolerated each other. We both had big eyes and long hair but Punkin was very quiet but had the funniest laugh.

When these episodes would occur, I don't recall any of us really talking about it. Or maybe we did, but I don't remember. However, back then it wasn't uncommon for people not to address the elephant in the room. I guess there really was no need because my mom would always go back to him.

One night I guess I was too wild while getting a spanking that my stepdad sat on my head and beat me. I say me, because his belt hit me everywhere but my face because he was sitting on it. I remember, my mom standing there yelling, "Don't beat her when you're mad!"

This memory has been painted in the back of my mind because I remember thinking, why is he beating me anyway? He ain't my Daddy! By this time, I hated him; and I think he knew it. I'm not sure if it was how he would treat my mom or when his one and only precious daughter would come into town for the weekend, he would put on this act as if we were all the perfect family.

I never forgot the day I learned that he had never laid a finger on his daughter. She never got popped in the mouth, on the hand or a slap on the butt with a belt. I could never really wrap my mind around this because I was getting beatings that left bruises, being made to hold a pitcher of salt for hours with my hands straight out (while family members laughed and took pictures of me) as a form of punishment. I also had to "bob" for hours when I did something wrong.

In case you are wondering what "bobbing" is, it's when you squat down where your butt is almost on the floor and you slowly come up and then down and up and down like your bouncing, but it was called "bobbing." I had to do this for hours at times when I had gotten into trouble.

One night my mom and stepdad invited another couple and their kids over. My stepdad and the guy worked together so my mom and the lady became best friends; well that was until she later learned that she was sleeping with my stepdad behind my mom's back.

I had accidentally spilled finger nail polish on the floor and my stepdad saw it and made me come by the table where they were playing cards and made me "bob" right there for hours. If I ever lost my balance, I would get hit hard with the belt. So, you guessed it? I became the master "bobber." Whenever I was done though, my legs would literally feel dead.

I remember "bobbing" at the table with four adults sitting there, waiting on three of them to rescue me.

But no one said nothing; including my mom. It was as if it had become the norm. My mom was laughing and playing cards with her friends and either didn't care (how I felt at the time) or was too scared to come to my rescue.

Another punishment was that I would have to come home, do my homework, chores and then straight to bed. No tv or nothing. Of course, my sister used to let me stay up until he got off work. My mom worked nights and my stepdad got off at 5pm or so. I always remember the house feeling extremely cold when he came home.

He would literally walk through the house and touch weird things like the top of the ceiling fan, or the back side of a vase or on the top of the fireplace just to make sure we did everything we were supposed to do. My sister and I got to the point that we stopped vacuuming the floor until it was close to the time for him to get off because we had gotten into trouble so many times for him not being able to see any vacuum marks.

We literally were like slaves. How could my mom leave us home with this man? I remember my sister and I room was right across from each other. Every now and then she would surprise me and come into my room but most of the time she would be in her room. I would beg her to keep her door open. She did. This made me feel close to her because most of the time I was scared to death because I literally got in trouble for everything. My sister rarely got into trouble.

I was this hyper active little girl who was being physically abused by her stepdad and rarely saw my mom because she worked all the time. We would always have really nice things though. I wasn't really into name brand back then so my mom would dress me in colorful yet girly outfits. I had every color Keds. There was a lime green pair I remember to be exact.

It wasn't until I was in my twenties when I told my stepfather's daughter how he treated us and all we had been through. She cried like a baby saying she had no clue. Growing up she was like my real sister. In my eyes, it was three of us. We had so much fun when she came over on weekends. I first met her when she was about two and all the way until our twenties is when we parted. The weird thing was my sister and I were four years apart and my stepdad's daughter and I were four years apart. Sisters. That was us.

Growing up my sister would make up rhymes for us and I remember they would be so lit! We named one song, "Make up Your Mind." Me with my silly self would sing the hook (I always loved to sing although I couldn't-LOL). I switched it up Jamaican style and it sounded a little like this:

"Make up your mind mon, make up your mind mon, make up your mind mon, make up your mind!" I'd repeat that while my sisters were super hype

around me and then I'd begin to adlib to make it even hotter. Those moments with my girls were priceless.

Prior to my stepsister and I separation, we had vowed that when either of us would get married, we'd be one another's maid of honor. Well, she's married now with a new "son-in-love" (I despise the word "step" except in this case I am mentioning above) and I wasn't invited to the wedding.

It all happened after I came out and shared with her what happened, and she sympathized with me. But when I shared with her in 2014 that I was including this part of my story in the book, there suddenly became a problem.

I can recall us talking via email and she sent me the longest, meanest message ever! She called me a victim and told me I was trying to change the way she viewed her dad.

As tears fell from my eyes. I remember typing, "I'm sorry that the man you have known to love is an angel to you. But he was a nightmare to me and my family." I went on to share how I know it was hard to hear and accept especially with her being his only child. But I assured her that it was true. It happened, and it kept happening.

It was in that moment I was officially cut off. After growing up with her, traveling to not one but two graduations, going to visit her multiple times when she relocated to nothing. "So, now we are not sisters no more?' is what I thought immediately after. Well I guess not. I never heard from her again; that I can recall.

Sure, I came across her on Facebook a few times until I was blocked. Then, I found her on Instagram and saw her new family. I remember instantly feeling very happy for her until I saw the photo of her with her Dad. I knew he was the one who got into her ear. He was the reason my life was so jacked up and now I no longer had my sister. But hey, that's her Dad. What was I supposed to do?

With all that's going on in the news right now with the recent R. Kelly trial, I can only imagine what his children (especially his daughters) are facing. People are facing real pain and it doesn't care if you are unknown or well known. Everyone is hurting from something; we all just cope differently.

So, trust me, I've experienced hurt and betrayal from women claiming to be my sister, way before the Trinidad experience that you may or may not have heard about. That is only a small part of my story. It's always interesting to me how people will create a story just to have one.

That's why I chose to share mine. I am no longer afraid. My intention is never to hurt anyone, but I free myself as I talk about what I've gone through. My story runs so deep that I've honestly considered writing a novel and creating characters because it's really that crazy that you may not even believe me if I told you some of this stuff.

Some things I've done have been down right embarrassing. But hey those are parts of my life as well. Never be ashamed of where you've been especially if you no longer reside there. But even if you do, commit to becoming a better you, seek help in order to overcome. No one is too far gone to snatch back their life and impact the world!

Harboring unforgiveness prevents you from becoming your best self. Release the hurt and lay it at the feet of Jesus! Trust me, He can handle every ounce of your truth!

Chapter Two

Pregnant at 17

I never imagined that I would have a daughter. Honestly, it wasn't a desire of mine. Growing up my mom would always tell me that I would get back the things I had done to her when I had my own child. She scared me to death saying things like that!

Therefore, having a child was never on my list. I was like oh no! I had done some stuff and I didn't want a repeat from my daughter.

But then I met this guy when I was sixteen and he was twenty-one. I think I was working at Kentucky Fried Chicken during that time and he had come through the drive through smiling all hard.

Long story short, we began to date and eventually he asked me to be his girl. Back then that's what guys did when they wanted you to be their girlfriend. So, we were officially dating and began sexing all the time.

It's like he had to have it every day and I was there giving it to him. He eventually ended up moving into my mother's home with me. You read this correctly. I was sixteen with a live- in boyfriend.

When I began dating him, he started buying my school clothes, and shoes so of course my mom loved him. The more he did for me, the less she had to do.

However, what my mom didn't see for a while was how much we used to argue. He had a very strong personality and so did I. He liked things his way and I liked things my way.

GRANDMA TOLD ME SO

Everyone just knew we were going to get married. I remember one day my sister's grandmother who is a pastor called me into her bedroom and said she wanted to talk to me. She told me, "Baby, I know you don't want to hear this, but..."

She then took a long pause and told me "He is not your husband." I remember laughing in her face because to me she was old, and her stuff had cob webs on it. I have to admit though, she was the cool grandma that you could talk to about anything and she would keep it straight with you. However, when it came to dating I had never seen her with a man so it was hard for me to take her serious in that area.

But it was my sister's grandmother, Bishop Ella Grimes who taught me how to pray, fast, and make God a priority in my life. I'll never forget it. I grew up going to a little small white church that sat up on a hill called Miracle Deliverance Holiness Center. That's where I was taught the Word of the Lord and what it meant to have faith in God.

MDHC was also the place where I spoke publicly for the first time when asked to speak on the fruit of the spirit.

Although I trusted her as my spiritual leader, I did not think she had a clue what she was talking about when she said my boo thang that I thought I was madly in love with, wasn't my husband, I couldn't receive it.

But boy was she right except it would take me a few years to realize it. So, we dated, and he was a really, good guy. He took good care of me, bought me whatever I wanted. However, those things had a down side to it.

Although I could drive his car to school sometimes, I could only go to his mom's house or back home to my mom's house. Then it grew to the point that if I was at this mom's house too much while he worked, he didn't like that. So, I just stayed home.

During this time, I don't remember having friends around like that because he became my whole world. After I came home from school, did my homework, ate; etc.; I found myself washing, drying, folding and ironing his uniforms for work. I was also cooking dinner and having it ready for him by the time he got off. (Remember, I was only sixteen doing all of this.)

I was literally following the encouragement of my mom. As long as I kept him happy, I'd be good. I am not upset with my mom for teaching me this, I just feel we teach others according to what we know at the time. She could only give me what was in her to give. So, I took it and ran with it.

HOW DID THIS HAPPEN?

There I was sixteen-seventeen years old with a live-in boyfriend. Early on he would share how he always wanted a family and he would share his childhood stories of how he wanted to be a great dad to his children; etc.

After so many conversations like this, he convinced me to have his baby. We began having unprotected sex with hopes of getting pregnant. I remember times when he would hold my legs up in the air (as if that would help) but I never got pregnant.

One day we got into a bad argument and I threw his clothes out in the street, broke all the crystal his sister had brought him back from Germany, and scrubbed all of his Timberland boots across the street and left it all out there.

I'm sure you are thinking, "What the heck did he do?" I don't even remember. What I do recall is how for a slight moment I literally had lost my mind. I don't recall him cheating on me ever (unless he did and I didn't know about it,) but it was one of our silly arguments that had gotten out of hand.

I remember when he came home and saw all his stuff outside, he flipped out but then I got mad when he tried to drive-off, so I took something and hit his windshield.

Let's pause, ladies why do we do stuff like this? You claim you want him to leave, so you throw all his things out, but when he tries to leave you get mad and try to stop him. Sound crazy right? I see I am not the only one that has lost my mind before.

So, he gets out of the car and although he would never hit me, he picked me up and slammed me on my mom's concrete driveway. This is how I know I wasn't in my right mind because my back should have been broken. But I jumped right back up and ran after him again.

I guess he realized, this girl is crazy. He jumped in his car and sped off. I am not too sure all that happened during this break up, but I do recall it being six months and I didn't see him one time during our split.

Although he simply did what I asked, I always wondered why he didn't fight for me. Was I not worth it? Did he no longer want me? Was it because I couldn't get pregnant? What the heck was wrong with me!?

GOTTA GET MY MAN BACK

During this time, I learn he is dating a girl from my high school. I was smooth back then, so I became friends with the girl, and she was silly enough to tell me all their business. I talked all this hooblah about how I didn't want him, and she believed it. We started hanging out and I was playing her so badly.

I knew he wouldn't stay with her long if she was friends with me. That was the point; to break them up. Silly rabbit. Did she really think I was going to sit back and watch her brag about the clothes and shoes her "new boo" bought her when those were the exact same things, he now no longer did for me? Absolutely not! I had a plan and it was going to work!

Funny thing is she would come back and tell me how he told her she was crazy for even being friends with me. Now that I think back, I feel bad because to this day when she sees me it's still awkard all because I re-stole my boyfriend back from her.

One day I received a call or text from his cousin who was more like his sister asking me to come over. I found it odd, but I went. A little after I arrived, he showed up all smiles and charming as ever.

I can't lie, I was so happy to see him. We made love that night like no other. I was seventeen years old and had visited the wild side for a short time due to having my heart broken. I had even messed with one of his friends out of hurt. Well, he wasn't really his friend, but he was a guy he knew, and they were "affiliated." My silly self was the type that whoever I slept with, I felt so in love afterwards especially if it was good. How naive.

After we made love, I remember him looking into my eyes asking what I was doing out in the streets. He was like, "I know you're not a hoe so why are you acting like one?" Word travels fast I see. This little small town, I knew he was bound to find out.

I remember crying and shaking my head as to say, "I don't know." I felt even worse because I had got up with an old friend who had just got out of prison the night before. That was the worse experience ever. He wasn't circumcised and I was traumatized for life. It wasn't until I was older that I learned what comedian Mike Epps meant when he did the "turtle neck" joke. How disgusting!

I remember him hugging me and telling me he loved me. We held each other that night and went to sleep at his cousin's house. We talked here and there afterward but that was kind of it. I always wondered 'why did he call me over there?' Just to have sex with me and go back to the girl he was dating at my high school?

Some weeks went by, then a month and I missed my period. At this point, I wasn't thinking anything because I was convinced that I couldn't have children being that we had tried so many times to no avail.

I don't recall all the details in between but what I do remember is when I found out I was pregnant and how far along I was, I did the math to a tee and knew the other guy couldn't be the father.

I've always been a very honest person (sometimes too honest), therefore, when my "back on" again boyfriend asked me if I was messing around with someone else I reluctantly but honestly told him yes.

I explained the situation and told him who it was (mistake number one) and how it all went down (mistake number two). What I should have done was just answer his question. My mom always told me that I talked too much. "Just answer exactly what someone asks you and nothing more."

Somehow, it got back to his family that I was messing with this other guy which wasn't true because it only happened one night, and he was let's say a little challenged so technically nothing transpired really. But again, they could have heard it from other people because I came out of my shell for a bit during our break up.

I remember his mom saying that's not my grandbaby; like she literally said this to me. I was so hurt because I always thought I was close to his family, however, this moment revealed that things weren't the way I had thought after all.

Immediately after he learned that I was pregnant it's like he wanted to be with me again. We got back together, and he was amazingly supportive my entire pregnancy. He would purchase maternity clothes for me and all types of gadgets to hear our baby's heartbeat. He was the over the top Dad seriously.

He kind of reminds me of how Rapper Papoose (husband of rapper Remy Ma) is with their new baby whom he nicknamed, "The Golden Child." Just over the top. LOL

He would kiss and rub my belly all the time. Like literally I couldn't stand him most of my pregnancy. For some odd reason I kept a yeast infection and he didn't care, he still wanted it like every night. There were so many times he went in did his thing and I was literally halfway sleep just waiting for him to finish.

He would place headphones on my belly so our new baby could hear the music. Feeling her kick for the first time was the most memorable moment of my life. She was suddenly all I cared about.

During this time, the comment his mom made to me often replayed in my mind, "That's not my Grandbaby." I will never forget those words. They made me second guess myself so much that I prayed every night that God would allow my daughter to come out looking just like him to shut all the haters up.

I admit I had made some mistakes but dang I knew who my child's father was. When I say I prayed every night, I prayed every night.

One time I almost thought I was going to lose my baby because my now ex-friend (his ex-girlfriend) jumped on me at my locker when she found out he and I were back together. I never found out how he cut it off with her, but she knew I was pregnant and immediately when she attacked me, I protected my stomach. I never hit her back although the fight was over quickly. She was much bigger than me and I would tease him by saying things like, "So you like climbing mountains now I see."

Come to think of it, I still owe her a butt-whooping for that. But I've been redeemed by the blood of the Lamb. Ok, Jesus just saved yo' life boo boo kitty so I'll let you slide on out. LOL

MY PREGNANCY JOURNEY

As time grew closer my doctor began to share with me how I wasn't dilating therefore, they gave me Pitocin to help soften my placenta and something else that caused false contractions.

My pregnancy was amazing up until this point. I only had morning sickness a few times, I didn't begin showing until about five months. I waited until my ninth freaking month to get stretch marks which was totally my fault because I was silly enough to say, "I don't even have stretch marks!" Well, the stretch mark demon heard me because it was as if they appeared everywhere what seemed like overnight.

It was December 3, 2002 (my initial due date) and I'm back at the hospital only to be starved and able to eat ice chips for 24 hours as I endure these false contractions. In my mind at eighteen, I'm thinking, so I'm laying here hurting for no reason. I already felt so ugly being pregnant. My nose was already big so it was stretched wide across my face, my breast were huge and I couldn't fit any of my clothes, my neck was as dark as Michael Blackson. It was just awful. Lol

After having doctors coming in and out checking my cervix one would say, "You've dilated one centimeter," and the other one would say, "You haven't dilated at all." This was the most vulnerable space I had ever been in. My legs cocked wide open for all to see my business. Thanks a lot baby daddy.

Finally, they gave up and decided to schedule me to have a c-section. I remember being so scared because I didn't know what to expect and I was terrified of needles. I remember my mom getting upset with me because I could only have one person in the room with me while I delivered my daughter and she expected it to be her.

All my boyfriend kept saying was, *"I'm going to see my daughter being born."* I was like, *"Ma, it's his baby."* With a straight face, she looked at me and said, *"You're my baby."*

THE ARRIVAL OF MY ANGEL

On December 11, 2002 at 11:56am I gave birth to a baby girl, Patience Armoni Harris. She was 6lbs, 6oz and was 19inches long. She was my pride and joy. I did it! I had a baby. I was now a woman. Or so I thought.

I'll never forget the look on her dad's face after the doctors finished playing tug-of-war in my belly and she came out. He cried like a baby. I remember him being so happy.

Patience's Dad was there with me through the entire pregnancy. He made every doctor's visit and one time he wouldn't leave the hospital room and I had to beg him to go get something to eat just so he could get out. He was so afraid of missing any special moments (as he called them) that he would eat the food they would bring me. LOL That wasn't barely anything, but I guess it was enough for him.

The first time I looked into my daughter's eyes I remember feeling a warm sensation run through my entire body that I had never felt before or could ever imagined. She was so beautiful and guess what else? She looked like a replica of her dad.

God had answered my prayers! Wow! That's when I really knew God was real because baby when I tell you that child looks just like that man, she looks just like him! I often joke with her and tell you, "You look like your Dad but you're pretty because of me."

It was my daughter's father who encouraged me to breastfeed and I did until I got mastitis in one of my breasts and boy did it hurt! Mastitis is inflammation of the breast and basically my milk was clogged up and it hurt like heck to get it out.

He would rub my breast for twenty and thirty minutes at a time to help relieve the pain. I remember being in the hospital trying to pee in the pan while being pregnant and he was always clowning. I literally couldn't stand him most of my pregnancy.

I'm trying to pee, I need him to hold my hand, I have a needle in my other hand and he's recording the moment. Talk about being pissed off? I was at the highest level of pissivity (yes that's a word; I just made it one.) He thought it was so funny and I was mad as fire.

Thinking back now as I write this book, I paused to share this story with my daughter, and she laughed. I don't think I ever told her about this. It's funny how you remember certain things as you reflect over your life.

Breastfeeding Patience was painful but helped me lose the weight quickly. She would always fall asleep while feeding and when I tried to lay her down, she would wake back up. My mom used to joke and call her a "Titty baby." LOL But I honestly feel that's what bonded us. She was on my boobies a lot. Until of course Mr. Mastitis interrupted our flow.

I admit I was kind of glad but did not welcome the pain because I could finally do something else instead of having a baby hang on to me all day by my chest.

After giving birth to Patience I was diagnosed with post pardon depression. I remember not really wanting to hold her right after giving birth to her. Someone had to be at the house with me to help me with her because I literally could not move around. It felt as if my abdomen was detached from my stomach and I walked around humped over afraid as if I would tear something.

I always felt Patience could feel my sadness of what I was going through because she didn't smile until she was a month old. I was glad when that moment was over for me because I quickly enjoyed holding her, feeding her, dressing her, rubbing my nose against hers and I never wanted to put her down.

THE MOMENT THAT CHANGED EVERYTHING

Things quickly took a turn for the worst while enjoying my new baby and adapting to my new life of motherhood. For whatever reason her Dad and I could no longer work whatever issues we had out and I honestly believe he broke up with me (can't really remember, you know back then it was important who broke up with who.) But in my mind, it was simple, we had broken up.

I felt so trapped and betrayed. You begged me to have this baby now I'm finally pregnant and you leave me? I had no idea how to cope.

Things were so bad between us that my mom had to mediate. He wouldn't communicate with me at all. I think we started out where he would get her every weekend. This was great for me because I could drink and party with no baby to worry about.

I guess he started hearing I was living my best life and quickly shut that down. LOL Then he switched to every other weekend. That was fine too because I simply stayed in when I had her and turned all the way up when I didn't.

I always prided myself on the number of guys I had around my daughter and I never moved a man into our home outside of her father. That was non-negotiable. After being physically abused by my stepfather I refused to allow any man outside of her father to tell my daughter what to do or even feel as if he could discipline her. That was a no-no.

Unfortunately, the ball wasn't played the same on her daddy's end of the court. What felt like just a few months later, her Dad got involved with a Caucasian woman whom I had zero issues with, however, I admit I was hurt because I was so in love with him (or so I thought.)

Since he wanted to go and date a white girl, I decided to go put his butt on child support. This really made him mad. I admit I did it out of hurt and pettiness like a lot of women do. Because truth be told he's always been a great provider and amazing father. We didn't flow well together as a unit, but I was young and didn't know how to channel that energy. So, I took it with me down to the Division of Child Support Services.

I don't even think it really mattered that she was white, honey she could have been Mexican, Latina, or even another black girl and I still would not have liked it.

As Patience grew older; she was maybe around two or three, I think. I am so bad with ages I more so remember details rather than time frames, but she was young. I was a member of her Grandfather's church in Robersonville, NC. Her dad wasn't going to church at that time. However, Patience and I would go faithfully. When her father learned of this suddenly, him and his new girlfriend began coming and guess where they would sit? Right behind me.

Her dad would have this rule he created that I was not to speak or address Patience if she was out with him. During this time, he knew he could control me. I basically did whatever he told me to do for years as we raised Patience.

That's all anyone ever talked about was how blessed I was because they saw how much he bragged about her on Facebook. I honestly believe he used that technique to draw other girls to him so they could say, "Awwwww, he's such a great dad. I'm sure he will be so good to me!" Yeah right!

What everyone didn't know was behind closed doors he was making my life a living hell. I'll never forget all the times he and his girlfriend would come and sit right in front of or behind me at church and I would be trying to focus on the service and tears would fill up in my eyes. I honestly felt hopeless. No one to really talk to about it so I held it all in. That's why I was so angry and slept with guys that I cared nothing about. Because my heart was bleeding, and I would do anything to get it to stop.

I remember being in the mall one year on Halloween night and this guy had my daughter in a blond wig dressed up as Miley Cyrus with black eye liner under her eyes.

I saw my daughter and my heart immediately went out to her, for one that awful costume but also because she was my baby. But we were both well trained. She saw me, I saw her, and I walked right by.

Yep, I know you may have all kind of curse words going on in your head right now as you read this. I didn't know any better. I thought I was to do whatever he said so that's what I did.

I had to deal with hearing my mom come home talking about "Mommy _____ (her name) this, and Mommy _____ (her name) that. It did kind of grow on me though because I noticed how much my daughter loved her.

I could tell he had filled his girlfriends' head with all kind of nonsense about me because she was always very standoffish and sometimes even rude to me. But I was there to take it all. I had been so hurt by this point that I was numb.

Funny thing is I always knew he wouldn't marry her though. I can't explain how, but I just knew it. I honestly always felt he wanted to get back with me but because he had spoken so bad about me publicly his pride wouldn't let him. Sadly, I would have taken him back. I didn't want to be a "baby mama" raising my kid as a single mother. That sucks!

Two years after Patience was born his girlfriend got pregnant and out of all the names in the world, they had to dig into the name he and I had for our son if we had one. We would have named our son, Jhabriel Elijah Harris and I guess he liked the middle name so much he decided to name his son that.

I was extremely hurt, betrayed and clueless as to why he would want a name that was a part of me. Out of all the names in the world this is the best you could come up with?

FURTHER BETRAYAL

I've been through so much in my life that sometimes I must pause and give God glory that I made it through it all. We as people have our individual stories that make us who we are today. Despite it all I wouldn't take any of it back. Why? Because I wouldn't be writing book number ten and wouldn't have such great content to share with you guys!

Being a teenage mom was tough. I went through a lot of things as I was trying to find myself and even worse, I now had another life I was responsible for.

During this time, I began dating women and I remember my daughter's father trying to humiliate me by taking me to court to take my daughter away from me. He didn't agree with my lifestyle and he wanted everyone to know it.

I was very young sitting in court all alone, no one to go through this with me and the unspeakable happens. In walks his dad, my pastor and sits on his side during our court case.

My heart dropped. How could pastor stand with him when he is doing all these bad things to hurt me? But hey that taught me a valuable lesson, at the end of the days, folks can love you, but they are gonna ride with their family when it comes to choosing you over them.

The Lord was on my side that day although I had to sit through him lying on me telling horrible stories that literally made no sense. What topped it off was when he had his son get on the stand and lie about me coming to their car door with a knife.

I couldn't believe what I was hearing. We did get into an argument and because I had so much anger built up toward him from the years, I allowed him to control me, I admit I did act out of character. I jump out of my car and went to approach him in his, but he locked the door. However, there was no weapon of any kind in my hands.

The fact that he would do that hurt me to my core. I'm like what if these people locked me up. You have this cute as a button biracial kid on the stand saying the exact things his father has prepped him to say.

The judge denied his argument for full custody because he found me not to be a danger to my daughter. That's a scar I have by him that will last for a lifetime.

I never understood how two people could love each other so much and then the minute they break up all hell breaks loose. The only way I could describe all that I went through with him is he basically did to me what most "baby mamas" do to their baby daddies.

The only thing I could think to do was to put him on child support but that was pretty much it. He controlled me for many years after that. Whatever he said I basically went with.

It wasn't until one year I read, Managing Your Emotions by Joyce Myer and I learned that he knew me from the inside out and the only way he was able to control me was because he knew what my exact triggers were. So, I had to change my responses to them.

I slowly began to change my reactions to him by not responding in angry outbursts like I used to. One time I stood up to him and told him, "No more! I've let you control me long enough! This is my daughter and what I say goes!" I had no more problems out of him after that.

It was almost like when Angela Bassett's character who played Tina Turner fought Laurence Fishburne's character who played Ike Turner back and I mean she got him good. Most of us watching it was like finally! That's what my moment was like. I felt like dag, I should have did this a long time ago!

But what happened was I stopped listening to my mother and decided to stand up for myself. No longer was I going to allow anyone to control me.

Today my daughter's father and I get along a lot better. I've learned with him not to overdo it, don't talk too often and keep it simple when I do. That's how we vibe. Patience is currently sixteen years old and honestly, it wasn't until she was around fourteen when we could have a sensible conversation without my mom's involvement.

I ended up shutting that down too. I told them both that I was sick of having to speak through my mom and that we were two adults, and this was our child and I was done communicating through her. I stopped and he had no choice but to speak to me eventually. His argument was always, Patience will grow up eventually and I'm like yeah and when she does, I pray she doesn't remember how you tried to keep her away from me.

The purpose of sharing these stories is not to make my daughter's father look bad but to share my truth. These are things I went through as a young woman. I did some crazy things and some still affect me today, but I've grown and developed into a better woman and mother and he's evolved into a better man and father.

Simply put: Lust (not love) will have you acting all kinds of crazy. We were two young people who thought we were in love and ended up with broken hearts and lashed out at one another.

I told someone the other day that we are family. This man gave me the greatest gift ever and that was my daughter. Without him she wouldn't be here, so I'll love him for the rest of my life for that.

You must understand how big that is for me to say that because I'm the same woman who used to pray every night that God would kill him because he was making my life miserable. For this, I often thank God for unanswered prayers.

Pain can take you to the lowest of the lows and have you doing things you never imagined you'd do. Healing is essential to our lives. We must extend forgiveness to others as well as ourselves and try to understand why people do the things they do.

Never despise your pain for there is purpose hidden within it if you'll commit to doing your soul work in order to discover the mystery of who you really are who lies under all you have been through!

Chapter Three

In Search of Love

Not everyone knows what it feels like to have a hole in your heart in which nothing can fill it with an exception of the very thing you've longed for all awhile.

Growing up with my Dad struggling with alcoholism and being in and out of my life has left the deepest scar I have ever encountered. Not only did I try to fill it with things, people and activities but I also tried to fill it with sex.

Over ten years ago, I was in the lowest place of my life. By the age of 24 I had experienced things that some women in their 50's hadn't been through. In that process I didn't have many people I could trust with my secrets therefore, I kept them to myself.

Many days I would write in my journal as my tears would land on the ink as I emptied the depths of my soul. I would 'tell God all about it,' as the old folks would say.

I remember being so frustrated with church, their lingo and their antics. I grew sick and tired of hearing the church mothers tell me, "Baby, God will keep you if you want to be kept." Sure, that's easy for them to say, they were close to seeing Jesus! All they had has now dried up and cracked.

Everything I had was still working properly and my hormones were all over the place! But who could I run to? There were times I tried to talk with spiritual leaders, but they would only judge me then drop me as if I was contagious or something.

I used to think I was the only one who dealt with this until one day a song came on the radio and it was Kelly Price saying, "I had a problem, and I asked you to pray..." She went on to share how instead of praying they talked about her and basically left her for dead.

It wasn't until that moment that I realized, wow celebrities are real people too and none of us are exempt from the jacked-up things that happen to us in life.

No amount of money can pay cancer to go away. No amount of people can heal the ache that's in your soul when the person you desire the most is the furthest away.

I can remember several instances while in my search of love and being accepted I ended up involved with a few married men. At the time I knew it was wrong but honestly, I cared nothing about their wives. I was like Positive K only my rendition was, "What your girl got to do with me?"

Sadly, I was once that girl who was clueless about sisterhood and failed to understand the law of sowing and reaping. Pain will lead you to do some very low things and I am not proud of any of them however, it is my truth.

One time I ended up with my Pastor's armor bearer. He was the worst lover ever, but he was fine and looked good on paper. I was young and I guess being involved with someone in power felt good. He drove a nice car, made tailor suits and always smelled amazing.

Oh, the price I paid for his company. We never went out on a date, unless you count my home as the meeting space. We would attend worship services and he would sneak and smile at me or make gestures that only I would understand.

In the back of my mind I wondered, if he could be the one. But then I realized, he couldn't satisfy me sexually. But he was cute though and we would look good together, is what I would tell myself.

Isn't it amazing the things we will do to satisfy people who don't have to go home with us at night? I grew tired of church folks telling me I needed to get married and how I'd make an awesome "First Lady." That's the language we tend to use in the African American community. Truth is, at that time, I didn't need to be anyone's first or second anything because my heart was wounded which often blurred my lenses and led to poor decisions.

One day I was in for a rude awakening. It came out that my pastor's armor bearer was married. Now, this was tough to grasp because when he wasn't with pastor, or running his business, he was with me; or so I thought. She never attended service with him, he didn't wear a ring, and no one ever referenced her; ever! (Unfortunately, it's a lot of that going on in the body of Christ today.)

So, what do I do? I had already had sex with him, so why stop now? I didn't want to add to my already long list of men I had been sexually active with. Ugh. I hated that feeling of...settling. That's what I did. I settled.

When I confronted him, this joker had the nerve to tell me he didn't think it was important because they were getting a divorce.

I'm like, so that's why you wanted to keep it silent and told me not to tell anyone because ni^*&a you're married! I'm just telling you how I said it ya'll. Don't judge me.

After I had enough and really wanted out but couldn't seem to tell him no although I was getting absolutely nothing out of whatever we had going on at the time. Learning about his wife and his response to not telling me made me feel awful. This time around I felt conviction therefore, I decided to go and talk with my pastor.

My intention wasn't to tell on him, but to free myself. Why did I do that? (rolls eyes) Well, the short version of that conversation is my pastor basically told me, "Why did you feel the need to have to tell me this?"

Blank stare. Wait, come again. You're kidding right? Nope, he was dead serious and sat there awaiting a reply. I was like well, I thought that's what I was supposed to do, come to you as my pastor for help.

I later learned that the real issue was that he didn't want to have to deal with it. After asking me a series of embarrassing questions such as how many times, did he use protection, and did I know about his wife, I was excused with a promise to "deal with him."

His "I will deal with him" promise basically meant he was sat down from his ministry assignments for about a week and was still Pastor's right-hand guy. That situation taught me that some leaders don't really care about the character of the people they have serving them, as long as they are loyal and look the part.

The weird thing was people not knowing he and I were dealing would tell me how much I favored his wife. They would say, "You look like the younger version of her," then they would call someone over to validate it. As I stood there extremely uncomfortable, I'd laugh it off and find a way to excuse myself.

This was after I found out he was married; or maybe they did know; nothing is usually a secret especially in the black church.

Then there was another incident and that was the last time I dealt with a married man because it was a hard lesson and pill to swallow. I learned quickly that

I had to deal with my pain another way because this wasn't it.

This time it was my team leader on my job. I don't even know how that happened, because I wasn't attracted to him. But after you work with someone everyday so closely you find things to like about them. He had nice hair, and hands, and he was tall. Yeah, he's tall; that's what I liked. SMH

As dumb as this sounds imagine how dumb I feel writing it. Please don't think for one second that it's easy to share my secrets but transparency is the best way to help people. I have experienced being called a whore and talked about. The only difference now is I'm no longer that person.

I also share my journey to help you recognize why you are doing some of the things you are doing. Most of the time our poor choices are stemmed from unresolved issues that left a hole in our heart and we are seeking something or someone (sometimes anyone) to fill it even it is only a temporary fix.

So, I become involved with my team leader, now this time, I knew he was married. But it's like it sort of happened. I don't know what kind of vibes or energy I was giving off but next thing I know we were in the back of the parking lot getting it on in his car during the work day!

I know that's terrible. The next thing it was car washes then my house. Now, the devil had a real plan for me because ya boy could do everything right. When I say everything, I do mean every-thang!

But that's Satan's tactics, to give you something that could eventually kill you, but you're blinded because it feels good to you.

The sad thing about my story is it wasn't until I became heavily involved in ministry that I got caught up with married men. When I tell you, I have been involved in more foolery in the church than I have anywhere else. That's why now I am very careful about where I go, and I am not moved by titles at all.

So...one day the condom broke. He jumped up, scared to death. I was surprisingly calm because I honestly felt I couldn't get pregnant due to abortions I had previously.

He is freaking out and saying here's $50 go get the morning after pill. Following what I was told, I do it and afterward I feel horrible. Maybe it was of the possibility of what might could have been. I had promised myself after my last two abortions that I wouldn't go down that road again. I felt terrible.

We slowed down a bit after that. Then here comes the guilt. I don't know why I suddenly felt like I needed to confess to someone when all the other stuff I had done previously I wrote about it in my journal and dared not to tell anyone but God (sometimes it's best to keep it that way!)

This time, I thought I had a friend. I'll never forget this girl who was a coworker and a supposedly sister in the Lord.

I confessed to her that I was messing with our team leader and she acted as if she was in my corner and prayed with me and even gave me advice on how to get out.

Little did I know she was a snake and the news were music to her ears but I didn't learn that she had told our supervisor until I was called into her office literally the next day or day after. Of course, I denied it and big mouth knew better than to come to work that day because I would have dragged her up and down that office building. But she was smart, she bared my secrets and then took a leave of absence.

He was the last person I wanted to face. I remember thinking, what have I done? It all felt surreal. After undergoing multiple pep talks with my married lover, he kind of kept his distance for a while. He would call, but that was only to see if I heard anything new. Then, he laid it on me. "Why would you tell the one person with the biggest mouth in the entire department?" I really thought she was a good friend. We had hung out, she used to bring me lunch from the dinner she cooked her husband the night before. This is why I'm so careful when it comes to eating other people's food.

I left all kinds of voicemails on her phone, but she wasn't responding, nor had she returned to work. The supervisor assured me they were doing all they could to keep it "in house" because they didn't want it to get back to his wife because she worked in another department. Really Carla? SMH

I continued to deny the accusations and went on to say how I didn't know why this young lady would make up these accusations. Honestly, she had no proof and it was my word against hers. Even when it came to the voicemails, I knew not to say too much and how to curse her out without using one single curse one (if you know what I mean.)

My supervisor stated she honestly didn't know what to believe but had to address it with him because it was brought to her office. From that day forward it felt like everyone knew when the truth is, they may not have.

I was embarrassed, already felt like a villain because the women there hated on me so much because they knew I had a life outside of work.

Oh, and just so we are clear, this incident occurred while I was in ministry. Yep, this was five years ago when I made what I felt was the biggest mistake ever, but God had a divine plan.

During this same time, I was already praying about leaving my job. I remember attending Woman Thou Art Loosed and received my breakthrough, then I came back and put in my two-week notice.

After the incident with oh boy, another guy from work would hit on me but I immediately shut that down because this situation had taken me through the ringer. I was done! Nobody else was getting in my bed or between my legs. Plus, he was married too!!!!!

We had even become good "work" friends, but I noticed he would flirt here and there, and I was determined to cut off the head of this demon that was ruining my life. If you are single, it's important that if you befriend a married man (or woman- this applies to men as well) that you try to have a relationship with their spouse as well especially if you two are identifying one another as friend.

Although God had Romans 8:28 my situation, it didn't come without multiple spankings. He beat my butt good and Satan had a field day with me from guilt, depression, anxiety and shame.

But through my pain I learned what it really meant to be a sister and a woman of integrity. My passion for sisterhood began to intensify and I increased the time I was spending in prayer and the Word of God.

From there I kind of left church folks alone. I found them to be the least loyal, and fakest people I had ever met. I realized after reflecting over my journey that most of the crazy stuff I ended up involved in was with people in the church (with an exception of the above incident.)

Most of the time it wasn't people in the world, but those that were praising God and hallelujahing and speaking in tongues that had the most issues.

It was then that I learned this attack really wasn't about me but the people that were connected to me in the spirit; some that I had yet to meet. Satan doesn't know all things, but he knows enough to try to derail us from our destiny in an attempt to destroy our life purpose.

My poor choices revealed the condition of my heart; it was wounded and so was my soul. At times I couldn't think properly. I would say yes, when I knew I should have said no. I would flirt when I really wasn't interested. Can you relate to this?

I would lay on the altar begging God to help me control my sexual desires only to go home and respond to a text that read, "Can I come over?"

Next thing you know I'm getting it in right after bible study. How the heck does that happen? Not caring for your wounded soul will have you doing all kind of weird things you never imagined yourself doing.

It wasn't until I watched this movie where this woman was battling a sex addiction when I realized that was the spirit Satan was trying to put on me. She kept having sex with people she really wasn't interested in and her husband was Boris Kojoe! Come on now!

I was also able to relate by watching TV shows such as Being Mary Jane where she would kick guys out after getting her fix.

More often than not, we as women struggle privately with so many things that we are too afraid to express due to what I experienced, someone having diarrhea of the mouth, or afraid of being judged.

Truth is, most people can't handle our truth that's why it's important for you to fully forgive yourself and others and nurture your soul wounds to heal them.

It wasn't until recently when I learned about soul wounds from my client, Dr. Tonya Cunningham. I had never heard that language before nor knew there was such a thing. But come to find out my soul was wounded and had been for some time.

The little girl within me had never healed properly and even in my late twenties she continued to cry out for help.

I overcame the struggle of feeling as if I had to have a man in bed or on my arm by divorcing religion and establishing a real relationship with Christ. I had to stop focusing on simply going to church and learn how to become the church.

The battles I've faced during my short time on earth is too deep to even share on any pages of a book. Some stories I'll never share because only God alone can handle my complete truth.

Same applies to you. No matter how much people say you can trust them, don't! Trust God! People always eventually disappoint even when they don't mean to.

Now, I am not saying don't develop healthy relationships but what I am saying is don't look for them to be God in your life because only God can handle the fullness of where you have been, who you are emerging into and where you are destined to be.

In your search of love, invite God into your brokenness. Whatever you have been filling it with has only deepened the emptiness you feel. Let it go. Let go of religion. Let go of that married man (or woman). Let go of that toxic relationship. Let go of the nicotine. Let go of the sex toys. Let it go!

I know it may be tough therefore, don't attempt this without prayer and fasting. Only a spiritually mature person will be able to handle your truth.

Be careful what you share with people, because once God delivers and elevates you there's always those whose lives haven't evolved that tend to remind you of where you once were.

Like the old folks used to say, "Take it to the Lord in prayer baby." My journal is called, "Letters to Daddy (Jesus)." I've learned to trust him with every part of my life even when I mess up. He knows all about me and yet he still calls me His.

The same applies to you. Your current struggle does not disqualify you from a life of purpose. Sure, God loves us too much to leave us the way we are, but the key is to focus on today and allow tomorrow to take care of itself.

I encourage you to consider therapy if your wounds are deep like mine once were (and sometimes still are) you may need professional help from a stranger who knows nothing about you and are bound by law with the contents of your session.

It's nothing to be embarrassed about. I recently hired a therapist and I am looking forward to getting to the root of my issues. I feel as if I've dealt with the symptoms for so long and now it's time to dig it up and cut the head off!

God uses people including a therapist who has a great couch for you to sit on as you unveil the depths of your soul.

Do your research, don't be in a hurry, be prayerful and trust God to see you through whatever you may be dealing with. If he can do it for me then surely, He will do the same for you.

By the way, I've told you a lot of my business so that makes us friends. Remember that!

God desires to fill every hole in your soul. Give yourself to him fully and watch Him mend the broken pieces.

Chapter Four

Mama's Baby, Daddy's Maybe

I've encountered painful experiences in relation to being teased growing up by my older sister with phrases like, "That's why Roscoe ain't yo daddy!"

Each time I heard those words it would pierce my soul and anger would arise within me, but I knew better than to try and fight my sister. She could do everything better than me so I knew she would whip my behind.

Until one day when she was pregnant with my niece (which was almost twenty years ago) and I had enough of her mouth, so I remember rushing her into the refrigerator and that was the first time I actually had fought back during an argument.

But I couldn't bring myself to hit her because after all, she was pregnant and how do you fight your own sister?

Well, clearly everyone doesn't think like me because just last year we got into a physical fight where I admit I mushed her in the face and she fought me like I was a chic on the street.

She had done something extremely foul and I wanted to pop off so bad but again, this is my big sister and honestly, I was more hurt than mad. But I ended up mushing her in the face and let's just say hmmm I got my tail whipped. I didn't fight back. When she grabbed my hair I in turn grabbed hers and that was about it. I was protecting my face the entire time.

Why did I share this? Wounds run deep when left unattended. We were kids when my sister used to tease me about my father and even now at 34 years old, I still have broken fellowship with him, and it hurts.

However, despite the pain I've managed to be okay and had to commit to my own healing journey and not focus on why others did what they did but instead focus on how I can work towards healing my triggers, forgiving myself and others (fully) and overcoming heartbreak.

I also had to remove unrealistic expectations of my parents to guard my heart and protect my environment.

CONFRONTING FAMILY SECRETS

While in the search of the truth I decided to go to my aunt (my mother's oldest sister) and ask her if My Dad really was my Dad? I knew if anyone was going to tell me the truth it was going to be her.

Boy did she lay it on me. It was as if she was waiting on me to ask her and then finally.... I did!

With a smile on her face, she said, "I really think Donald is your Daddy." She went on to share details about him. I always heard his name growing up but never knew what he looked like.

I ended up going to his mother's home only to be rejected by her because he basically took care of her and she didn't want to get in the middle of it.

But I could never get her out of my mind because when she opened the door, there I was laying eyes on someone who looked just like me. She was brown skin like me and had big brown, puffy eyes just like me.

I remember standing there speechless and quickly had to gather myself and tell her who I was while asking if I could come in.

She sat patiently and kindly listening to my story only to shut me down in the end. I did ask her if she would give him my information and she said yes although I had no expectation of her doing so.

He did call and invited me to come speak with him. I remember pulling up and he was sitting in the front yard looking totally unbothered.

Immediately when I saw him I grew angry again as I said to myself, 'I look nothing like this dude!"

There I was smack dead in a moment of confusion meeting the man I had heard of my entire life then when I see him there is zero connection in the physical.

He began to share how he knew about me and how my mom would always send him pictures of me and deep down he felt I was his daughter. He went on to say how at this point what was he to do?

"I'm about to get married," He said. Looking at him in disgust as to say, "Who gives a _____?"

People can be so selfish and only focus on themselves which leaves others heartbroken in the end and that is why I want to address family secrets in this chapter.

I have witnessed quite a few of my cousins grow up to think one person was their father only to learn years later that unfortunately such and such wasn't their Dad.

But do you want to know the worst part? Everyone knew except them? When are families going to stop sweeping things under the rug and deal with them?

That's the issue I have with my family currently. No one really talks about anything. Something can go on and depending on who it involves they will keep it quiet or "gossip" among themselves then move on as if nothing ever happened.

Well, I'm sure you can tell or have already discerned that I am the one that is the complete opposite. I'm the one that would be like, so umm let's address this before we move on to that.

My mom is also one of those people who can move on from a situation rather quickly. We can get into an argument today and she will text me tomorrow as if nothing ever happened. My attitude be like, "Wait a minute ma'am, I'm still mad!"

ANYWAY, BACK TO DONALD...

I remember asking him a very specific question, "Is there any possibility that I could be your daughter?" Without hesitation he responded, 'Yes."

He then went on to say how much time had passed and how he's getting married and blah blah blah.

I waited for him to finally stop talking and said, "I look nothing like you... Now on the other hand I look just like your Mom." I can't recall his response because I think I stopped listening to anything else he had to say after he pretty much told me, why did it matter if he was my Dad or not after so much time had passed.

The conversation finally came to an end and I remember leaving even more upset with my mom than ever before. Like, how could she do this to me?

I hate when parents do things to kids like they aren't going to grow up one day. Let that sink in...

During this time, I had the conversation with Donald I was working at Orthopaedics East and I received flowers from him which left me in further confusion.

He acted nonchalant when I was in front of him, yet he sends me flowers as if he has some type of sympathy for me all of a sudden. These were my exact thoughts at the time as I was picking the flowers up and throwing them in the trash.

They never made it to my car because that conversation was dead as far as I was concerned. I had been rejected enough and I was tired of taking myself through this downward cycle and battle with rejection and abandonment and feeling as if something was wrong with me.

I ended up having a conversation with my mom about meeting Donald and she seemed shocked that I would go to that extreme (as she called it). Each time I would talk to her about knowing who my Daddy was, or any issue for that matter, I would end up crying my eyes out while she would stand (or sit) there looking at me with zero bit of emotion on her face.

Honestly, I believe that's why I always had a love/hate relationship with my mom because it's like if she would show some sort of remorse, I could accept that. But then again, I try to understand what it may be like for her to have to relive her mistakes.

I guess I always wanted my mom to just come out and tell me the truth with no filter. You know? She knows everything about me, but I feel there are parts of her life that she doesn't unveil to me and I don't understand why. I'll continue to pray that one day we will have the conversation and the broken pieces will hopefully be mended back together again.

CONCLUSION

Parents tell your children the truth now, so it doesn't come back to bite you later. Trust me, they deserve to know. Yes, it may hurt, and they may be angry with you but at least you loved them enough to be integral.

I can recall working with a client who had a secret she had been holding since her childhood. She came to me to learn how to write and publish her book however, I found many holes in her story during the process of serving as her Writing Coach and Publisher.

"What is it you are not telling me?" I finally asked her. Silence filled the air for what felt like an eternity. She slowly shared how she was raped or molested by her mother's husband (or ex-husband) and became pregnant and her mother remained with him (if I remember correctly). Then the child grew up not knowing the man she called her grandfather was her father.

In my line of work (what I feel called by God to do) is much more than about business and profiting from our passion, it's about helping women (and men) emerge into who they've been predestined to be.

Professionally I would be considered a Life Coach, however, spiritually I see myself as a midwife; because I help women push beyond their limits and birth things, they never thought were imaginable. All of this takes place while providing them with tools and resources on how to heal in the processes and transitions of life.

Be careful when you tell God that you want Him to use you, because in order to help others you must first develop your own in the form of a testimony. You can not have a testimony without first encountering a test.

We all have our individual cross to bear and although it may be painful to revisit, sit your children down and tell them the truth. In the end, you'll be glad you did.

Why settle for the imitation when you can have the real thing in Jesus! No longer run to external factors in hopes of filling a void. Draw nigh to God and He'll draw nigh to you!

- *James 4:8*

Chapter Five

Nightmares at 23

I woke up and he was just standing there looking at us. What was he thinking? Was he thinking about killing us? I tapped my mom and pointed to him while saying "Look."

Trying to remain calm she told me to go to my room. I had begun sleeping with her since all the foolery with my stepdad. By now I was fully convinced that he was full blown crazy!

I had seen him take a 4x4 piece of wood and shatter the window of our glass sliding door when he saw my mom had a new boyfriend. By the way, that was the day I lost all respect for this guy. Sure, he was cool, but he ran just like the rest of us. Mom where did you find these guys?

Glass was everywhere and he chased my mom and threw her against the wall while grabbing on her clothes. I can't remember how old I was because it all seems to run together at times, but I do know from age 8-23 my life was quite interesting.

"Here!" I said, while giving my mom's new boyfriend a butter knife. "What am I supposed to do with this?" He yelled back! I was so scared that I grabbed the wrong knife. Well, first of all sir, why did you send me to get it anyway. Such a punk.

Those are the memories I have of my mom's second husband; my dad was her first.

I remember when he used to sit in his green recliner chair and hulk spit in a red plastic cup. It was so disgusting. To make things worse, I even caught him eat his buggers quite a few times. I mean, really, why would a grown man eat buggers? When I would see him kiss my mom, I vowed that she could begin to keep her kisses to herself and I'd settle for a nice hug.

As I mentioned in the earlier chapters, my mom worked nights and he worked days. We would see my mom before going to school and wouldn't see her again until the next morning.

Out of all the fights, there was one that changed my life forever. My mom and my stepdad had been fighting earlier that day and my sister went to bed with a knife under her pillow. Not sure what made my mom check, I guess it was her "Mommy-intuition" but she found it and asked my sister why she had it.

"Because the next time he hit you, I'm going to kill him," my sister blurted out. Now, I am not sure what was going on in my mom's mind during that time. But what I did know was that she was in her early twenties, on her second marriage, had two children (neither of us were his), and her mother had passed away.

Reflecting over, I can't imagine what life was like for my mom raising us while dealing with a cheating and overly jealous husband. When we wrote Redeeming the Time, I still didn't feel that my mom shared her story the way I felt she should have. I thought she would help bring insight to what I was feeling.

I guess I was being selfish, because I was still looking for answers so I thought if we wrote a book together, she would revisit her pain and share the story in writing. Instead, as she has done in previous conversations we have had, she downplayed everything and failed to acknowledge any of what I was sharing in my chapters.

Mind you, I wrote all my chapters first in our book, then my mom was to go back and read mine, then write hers. She said she read it but through her writings I couldn't really tell.

Sure, she shared during her childhood how her father would buy them things but wasn't fully present. That brought clarity in which it helped me understand why my mom wasn't very affectionate growing up (nor is she now) but would always buy us things which in her mind maybe she thought was making up for the things we lacked. But it didn't.

Although my mom and I have been through a lot she's still my favorite girl. My nightmares were all filled with terrors from my childhood and whenever I would learn she was dating someone new I would become extremely nervous, wondering what things were like when no one was around.

These thoughts derived from witnessing her second marriage. On paper, we were The Cosby Show, but behind closed doors we were Precious. My stepdad was both verbally and physically abusive and we all (including my mom) walked on pins and needles around him.

I ended up moving out of my mom's home when I was eighteen years old. I had recently given birth to Patience and my mom and I were bumping heads big time.

As time went on, I would have nightmares here and there that would scare the crap out of me. I have had one since my mom has been married to her now husband.

I remember calling her in the middle of the night one time, crying and hyperventilating and asking her if she was okay. I would dream that a guy she was dating would kill her or was beating her or even one time I dreamed that she went back to her second husband.

One time my mom asked my sister and I (she claim in a joking way) how we would feel if she went back to her second husband. My sister just gave her the most disgusting look and didn't say a word. Well, you know me with my mouthy self, I had to say something. "Go back to him and I'm done with you and I mean it," is what I told her with a straight face.

I then went on to ask her how the heck she could even consider doing some crap like that. That's when she claimed she was joking, and I was furious because nothing regarding him was funny to me at all. That's when I knew my mom was in complete denial about how he really tore our family apart.

Earlier I shared with you how my mom found the knife under my sister's pillow. Well, my mom ended up making my sister go live with her dad and I was left to remain in the home with this monster.

I was traumatized as a child and it led up to my adulthood. I almost hated men because of what I witnessed the men my mom dated do to her. One guy stole thousands of dollars from her safe and she did absolutely nothing about it, saying she couldn't prove it when all evidence led back to him.

It was a crazy time in my life, but you know what? I am glad it's all behind me now. I am not sure what happened at 23 but the nightmares just stopped. A period of time went by and I realized I no longer was having them.

But although the nightmares stopped the effects of the trauma were at an all-time high. I honestly never considered returning to therapy because of my experience as a child, (with Mrs. Simon Thomas whom I told you about earlier.)

We often hear of family cycles and generational curses and I believe strongly this is the case. I was often told that I was the younger version of my mom and that is why we bump heads so much.

When I thought about it. I was heavily repeating our family pathology; or should I say my mother's. She dated married men, and so did I. She was head strong as it relates to never relying on a man to take care of her and I became the same way.

I admit it was tough at first for me to allow a man to open the door for me because I didn't want him to get it twisted as if I needed him for anything no matter how small it might be.

Not to mention I had no clue this was what differentiated a gentleman from a man and that I deserved and was worthy of being treated as a lady.

One day I had to sit down and have a conversation with my mom about the things I was dealing with as a woman from PH balance issues to sexual struggles and I was delighted to know that my mom was open about some of the things she had done.

I would often joke with her by saying, "You the reason why I liked older men!" Sure, we would laugh but the truth was, it derived from my Daddy issues.

I liked a take charge kind of guy. I despised weak men.

All along though, I learned that I was a daughter in search of her father.

If you are someone whose past still haunts you, this is a great place for you to invite God in. I had to pray my way through every ounce of pain and dysfunction I experienced as a young woman even up to today.

There have been plenty of times where I have ended up in situations wondering, how the heck did I get here and why did I allow myself to do this again?

Don't beat yourself up sis (or brother). Just start paying attention to why you do the things you do, identify your triggers then work on healing them. We are all in a process and we must go at our own pace. With God on your side you are MORE THAN A CONQUEROR & indeed His BELOVED!

Your past has no right to haunt you when you have surrendered it all at the feet of Jesus. Give Him your burdens and exchange tragedy for triumph! Whether you believe it or not, you are an OVERCOMER!

Chapter Six

A Place to Belong

Many people today struggle with identifying where they belong in life as well as the Body of Christ (for those who are believers.) I can relate to this as well as within my family.

Growing up I wasn't popular (for anything good anyway) nor did I have a lot of friends. I tagged along with a few people where we hung out at "the spot" as a group but I was more of a one on one person.

I remember having a best friend, we called her Pamie. We would smoke weed at one of the guy's house in the neighborhood and I would steal my mom's van and go riding up and down the street as if I had somebody's license.

It's amazing the things you will do as a cry for help. I was hanging with the wrong people, wanting to fit in, wanting to feel wanted, loved and welcomed. I always felt as if her cousin didn't really like me but tolerated me because I was her friend.

Then, there was Shana, her and I were like sisters. We met and when she came to my high school, everyone thought we were sisters. Well, that was until she became friends with a group of girls who didn't like me, and they convinced her to no longer be my friend. I remember being so hurt to the point I wanted to fight her.

I could tell she didn't want to fight me and simply got caught up with the wrong group of girls and I guess I was outnumbered.

Come to think of it, I too was the "wrong girl," per my teachers because they would tell people not to hang around me because I was always getting into trouble.

Truth is, I often felt as if I had something to prove because I didn't really have anyone to protect me (not at school anyway.) My sister and I went to different high schools except one time when I think she failed her grade and I was a freshman and she was a senior and we went to school together briefly.

But we barely talked. There were times she would walk right by me like I wasn't her sister. I didn't realize until now how long this had been going on. Not many people knew she was my sister except those who lived in our neighborhood and saw us get off the bus together.

I don't recall us sitting together on the bus. At one time I felt my sister was embarrassed of me because I had to take medication and was always bouncing around.

There was a time in high school though when we did attend a basketball game together and this girl who had stolen my boyfriend from me was picking and my sister thought she was a grown woman and jumped on the girl after I kicked it off by punching her in the face.

So, it was moments like that where I was left confused because clearly, she had to love me to jump in a fight for her little sister. But why didn't she express it? Why did it often feel like she hated me?

I've struggled with feeling alone for a long time to the point I had to learn how to become comfortable in my own company. From church to my family I've never really felt as if I had a place where that was the perfect fit. It always seemed as if I was easily replaced by my friends as well as my family.

What helped get me through this was my relationship with God. I literally had become so disappointed by people that I had to go to Him and ask, "God who am I?"

I had grown to the point where I didn't like myself, but you couldn't tell that by how I looked on the outside. My hair was always done, apparel was always tight, but I felt broken and empty on the inside. I longed for a place to belong; somewhere to fit but sadly, I never found it until I surrendered and invited God in.

Now, I realize I have a place in God's Kingdom, and I don't have to seek validation from others but can allow God to be everything I need.

Today, God has sent amazing people into my life to love me, care for me and remind me of the impact I've had on their life.

Finding my place in the Kingdom came with first finding my voice and having the courage to share my story. I no longer held back my truth and where I had come from.

When I wrote my first book in 2014, I was surprised when it instantly became a #1 Amazon Best Seller. No gimmicks or schemes, I just released it and told people about it and guess what? They purchased it!

I had so many people leave amazing reviews on Amazon about how my book had helped them and how my story was a replica of theirs. If you go on Amazon right now and type in "The Power in Waiting- Carla Cannon, you'll see what I'm referring to.

Sometimes during my darkest moments I'll go back and read the reviews online to remind myself of the value God has placed within me and my specific calling in the earth.

No matter who you are or what God has done in your life, we all have a past that comes back to haunt us and try to fill our mind with negative thoughts of how unworthy we are.

I used to fall for this until I learned to turn feelings of unworthiness into worship. Truth is, none of us are worthy but because of Jesus, we have been redeemed.

No matter where you have been in life or where you may be right now, know there is a place for you, and it is in the Kingdom of God. So many are searching for peace which can only be found in the Prince of Peace: JESUS.

I am not trying to shove religion down your throat, but I am here to invite you into a relationship with Him. Having an authentic connection to Christ is what saved my life and keeps me getting up day after day.

If I couldn't pray, worship or study His word I'd be dead. Over the years I've found comfort and stability in the Word of God. I invite you to put more of an effort into growing your relationship with Christ than you do with the people in this world.

Unfortunately, as humans, we will all fail one another one day, but Christ He is unable to make mistakes. Everything he does is purposeful and all that he makes is good.

Be careful not to write yourself off because of the poor choices you've made in your life. Acknowledge them, own them and then commit to changing them.

If I can overcome, so can you!

You have a set place in the Kingdom of God, and don't you dare let anyone convince you otherwise! Not only have you survived your story and the pain of your past, but you are now about to thrive because of it! God doesn't call the qualified, but he qualifies the called!

Chapter Seven

Understanding & Healing the Father Wound

We all come into the world helpless, dependent and needing acceptance, to be treated as worthy, and to be blessed. The father wound is the absence of love from your birth father. The wound can be caused by:

- **Neglect** – I am unimportant
- **Absence** – Divorce, separation, death
- **Abuse** – Mental, physical, sexual, spiritual
- **Control** – Oppressive domination
- **Withholding** – Love, blessings and/or affirmation, deficiencies that lead to a profound lack of self-acceptance.

Let's be clear that a father can be present in the home yet unavailable emotionally to his children. I know many who have been affected by this and it is equivalent to growing up without my dad being physically in the home.

The effects of a father wound is low self-esteem, a deep emotional pain inside and a performance orientation that makes us "doers" rather than "beings." While salvation makes us new creations in Christ, it does not necessarily address this wound inside.

We tend to have four barriers that inhibit the healing of this wound:

- **Pride** – No will to confront or change, "I'm alright"
- **Sin** – A blocked will that neither seeks to confess sin or receive forgiveness
- **The wound itself** – Continuous emotional hurt inside
- **Lies** – Misconceptions about the self, birth father and Father God.

Instead of going to the pain and receiving the healing we need, we tend to respond to life events by creating a misconception about our "self."

Not having your birth father in your life can affect your personal identity especially when you are unsure of who you really are (lack of validation) or where you come from (unsure where your current struggles derived from).

There are people in the world who have never laid eyes on their father and there remains an emptiness that their spouse, children, job or extracurricular activities can fill.

RELATIONSHIP WITH OUR BIRTH FATHER

When we hold a conception of our birth father as angry, violent, uncaring, indifferent, distant/withdrawn, absent/abandoning, alcoholic, condemning and/or critical, we tend to believe the following words about ourselves:

- **I am unworthy**
- **I am stupid**
- **I am incompetent**
- **I am unloved or unlovable**

When we accept these words as truth, we will experience depressed, anxious and angry lives.

I grew up struggling with anger issues that when more closely assessed was a deeply hurt soul. I couldn't understand why my Dad didn't want me (or at least that's how I felt) and why he wouldn't fight to be in my life despite the differences he and my mom had.

As I developed and experienced adulthood I learned that parents are individuals who also grow up with their own soul wounds and the way society has trained many of us we developed a "what happens in this house, stays in this house" mentality.

Therefore, we shy away from therapy or seeking wise counsel on how to deal with what we are going through. Like me, I am sure you have heard the word "shrink" in relation to a therapist and were often led to believe something must be wrong with you if you need to see one.

RELATIONSHIP WITH GOD THE FATHER

Often a person's image of God the Father is contaminated by the personal experience he or she has with their birth father. When misconceptions about God are present (i.e. that He is angry, judgmental, unhappy with me, fearsome, legalistic, quick to punish and slow to forgive . . .) the words we tend to believe are:

- o **I am not good enough**
- o **I am guilty/shameful**
- o **I must work harder to justify myself**

When we accept these words as truth, we will seek to perform and prove our worth through perfectionism and materialism or seek addictions to cover up the pain.

This holds true for me. I believe that is why I have always been particular about how my home looks and have felt as if had to be on "point" anytime I stepped out of the house, regardless of what my soul looked like.

Isn't it amazing how we will spend tons of our hard-earned money dressing up our exterior, when our interior (the core of who we are) is left shattered? I too am guilty of this and agree that we all must do better.

ADDRESSING THE FATHER WOUND

There are four steps to addressing the father wound:

1. **Understanding the heart of God**
2. **Inviting Jesus into the wounds created by our birth father**
3. **Accepting the truth about one's self as a child of God**
4. **The heart of God**

(1)   One truth I had to come into the knowledge of is God is not like man (or anyone for that matter) and he gives each of us free will. Therefore, I had to be careful comparing my relationship with my birth father to my relationship with Him.

I also had to be careful not to blame Him when spiritual leaders disappointed or mishandled me (or others).

(2)   Next, I had to invite God into my brokenness because within His word I understood that only He could handle the totality of all I have been through in my life. Same applies to you.

You have a choice. You do not have to remain broken. Commit to doing the necessary work to overcome the pain of your past. Sometimes you must be selfish and intentional about focusing on yourself to nurture your soul back to life. There will always be someone to help; commit to helping yourself first.

(3)   Accepting that you are a child of God (THE KING) is essential to experiencing self-love. I am convinced that some people don't take care of themselves properly because we haven't been taught how to love ourselves.

Conversations are often centered around what we do for others and what we are contributing to this world. But God could care less. His concern is with us.

(4)   Knowing and understanding the heart of God is key to being a CHRISTian (being Christ-like). God is not like man that He should lie nor that He should have to repent. People will fail you, but God never will. He knew your end from your beginning and can handle *all* of it.

People say they want to know your truth and often encourage you to share it. I encourage you to be prayerful in doing so because there are a lot of wolves in sheep clothing.

God's love is unconditional (agape). I learned a long time ago that most people love you because of, however, God loves us despite our faults and failures.

Simply put, there is nothing like the love of God. I encourage you to embrace His love for you and don't settle for anything less than what God has to offer you.

SEVEN TYPES OF LOVE:

(According to www.pyschologytoday.com)

1. Eros

Eros is sexual or passionate love and is the type most akin to our modern construct of romantic love.

2. Philia

The hallmark of *philia*, or friendship, is shared goodwill. Aristotle believed that a person can bear goodwill to another for one of three reasons: that he is useful; that he is pleasant; and, above all, that he is good, rational and virtuous.

3. Storge

Storge ('store-gae'), or familial love, is a kind of *philia* pertaining to the love between parents and their children. It differs from most *philia* in that it tends, especially with younger children, to be unilateral or asymmetrical. More broadly, *storge* is the fondness born out of familiarity or dependency and, unlike *eros* or *philia*, does not hang on our personal qualities.

4. Agape

Agape is universal love, such as the love for strangers, nature, or God. Unlike *storge*, it does not depend on filiation or familiarity. Also called charity by Christian thinkers, *agape* can be said to encompass the modern concept of altruism, defined as unselfish concern for the welfare of others.

5. Ludus

Ludus is playful or uncommitted love. It can involve activities such as teasing and dancing, or more overt flirting, seducing, and conjugating. The focus is on fun, and sometimes also on conquest, with no strings attached. *Ludus* relationships are casual, undemanding, and uncomplicated but, for all that, can be very long-lasting.

6. Pragma

Pragma is a kind of practical love founded on reason or duty and one's longer-term interests. Sexual attraction takes a back seat in favor of personal qualities and compatibilities, shared goals, and making it work. In the days of arranged marriages, *pragma* must have been very common.

7. Philautia

Philautia is self-love, which can be healthy or unhealthy. Unhealthy self-love is akin to hubris. In Ancient Greece, a person could be accused of hubris if

UNDERSTANDING & HEALING THE FATHER WOUND

he placed himself above the gods, or, like certain modern politicians, above the greater good.

For further study you can also refer to the Word of God in I Corinthians 13:4-7 (New Living Translation)

4 Love is patient and kind. Love is not jealous or boastful or proud 5 or rude. It does not demand its own way. It is not irritable, and it keeps no record of being wronged. 6 It does not rejoice about injustice but rejoices whenever the truth wins out. 7 Love never gives up, never loses faith, is always hopeful, and endures through every circumstance.

As seen in the Prodigal Son story: (Luke 15:11-32)

- o we are free to choose our own path
- o the father waits patiently for us to return to Him
- o when we return, He accepts us unconditionally
- o He runs to accept and embrace us
- o He values us by celebrating God's provision for salvation
- o He loves us first
- o we are His beloved creation
- o He offers salvation for our sin
- o He wants a relationship with us

Jesus as the Wounded Healer:

- He was tempted by Satan to know our temptations
- He experienced suffering to know our suffering
- He was rejected, mocked, beaten and crucified
- He fully understands our pain and wants to help
- **1 Peter 2:24** "By His wounds you have been healed"

Jesus Heals:

- when invited into memories, He comes
- when He comes into memories, he is described as gentle, kind, caring, loving, warm, friendly, hugging, accepting and healing.

When you understand His love:

- confess to Him the misconceptions you have had
- receive His forgiveness
- receive His love

Invite Jesus into the wounds created by your birth father

Do inner healing for the memories:

- invite Jesus into the specific memories
- understand the words that you accepted at the time
- ask Jesus to reveal His truth to you
- receive His truth about who you are

Choose to forgive your birth father:

- for hurtful words
- for hurtful actions
- for not loving you
- for not blessing you
- for affecting your image of God, the Father

Accept yourself as a child of God

Receive the words of truth:

(I encourage you to write down the below affirmations on sticky notes or note cards and declare them aloud every day.)

- I am accepted
- I am chosen
- I am loved
- I am God's creation
- I am precious in His sight
- I am forgiven
- I have been redeemed
- I will never be left or forsaken
- I have an eternal inheritance
- nothing can separate me from the love of God

As you understand the truth about God's love and come to know your true self in Christ, it will free you to let go of the pain and forgive your birth father.

This new perspective created in you will now enable you to see your birth father through different eyes and allow you to live in freedom.[1]

Forgiveness is the key to moving on with your life and living out the purpose in which Christ created you. Although it can be tough, forgiveness is a must in order to experience the abundant life that is available to each of us.

One thing that helped me along my journey to healing and recovery is asking the right questions. Often times, we feel we are the only ones suffering when truth is, our parents grew up with their own issues, aches and pains from their childhood and also have soul wounds they may still be carrying.

Truth is, no matter how hard we attempt to prevent the reoccurring behaviors of our parents, when we do not know our history, we tend to repeat similar cycles as well as behaviors.

When I had my daughter, I quickly noticed my mother's voice hidden beneath mine. In order to break these cycles, I had to first acknowledge them. Next, I had to extend forgiveness and understanding because we simply do what we know to do even if what we know to do isn't what's best for those involved. Finally,

---

[1] (Article Reference: https://www.focusonthefamily.ca/content/understanding-and-healing-the-father-wound)

I had to commit to doing my "soul work" to begin the process to healing old childhood wounds.

Would you like to know the number one thing that caused me to submit to my healing journey? I grew tired of allowing the past to hinder my present. I would notice the very people who hurt me seemed to be living their best life while I remained stuck.

One day I was praying, and I cried out to God begging him to take away the spirit of anger. I was tired of allowing small things to set me off. I could literally be having a great day and someone I loved yet had unresolved issues with could say or do something that would set me completely off.

There comes a time in your life when you must make a decision to divorce anger and literally LET IT GO!!!! I know it may be tough, but you must grow to a place where you love yourself enough to implement self-love by detoxing your spirit of anger, unforgiveness, fear, doubt, and anything else that is preventing you from growing into the person you've been created to be.

Here are 10 Ways to Deal with the Pain in Order to Heal It:

1. Acknowledge your hurt
2. Reflect on the origin of the pain
3. Identify key players involved
4. Write out the specifics of what they did
5. Acknowledge the part you played
6. Give your heart permission to break
7. Extend forgiveness to yourself
8. Extend forgiveness to others
9. Extend forgiveness to God (yes, some people blame God for things that happen in their life)
10. Detox your spirit from all that has happened & utilize wisdom as you move forward in your life.

Chapter Eight

Healing Spiritual Parent Wounds

In six years of writing books, I have never found myself stuck when it came to a book project. I must admit I did my best to omit this chapter however, Holy Spirit continued to prompt me to engage in this conversation because there are so many people who have not only experienced soul wounds from their birth parents but their spiritual parents as well.

I personally have my own stories of being mishandled by leadership however, I feel led to share from a different perspective when it comes to such a sensitive topic.

Through my coaching agency I have been blessed by the opportunity to help women navigate through various situations as it relates to their spiritual, personal and professional life.

With all of the issues that tend to plague our communities, the one that was always the toughest was helping women overcome spiritual parent wounds.

I understand that not all leaders are bad however, we must not overlook the fact that some do prey on their "sheep" and manipulate them (especially women) into doing things against their better judgement. Unfortunately, it was my own personal experiences that taught me not to become so trusting because someone wears the title: Bishop, Apostle, Prophet or even Minister.

A person's title or function doesn't make up the totality of who they are, and truth is there are many wolves hiding behind these titles. I have been preyed on by men in the church however, when I reflect back, it was me who let my guard down because we went to the same church or he was my pastor's armor bearer, a musician or an important person in the local community.

I have also been "dropped" by individuals I believed to be spiritual leaders after I shared my private struggle(s) and it hurt me to my core.

I later learned that not all leaders are equipped to deal with every situation and sometimes the best way for them to handle a situation is to not handle it. Now of course to us it makes no sense, but some leaders believe so much in the power of prayer that they fail to recognize the power God has given them and instead they place all the responsibility on God.

I know what it feels like to have your spiritual leader look you in the face and say, "I don't know what to do with you." This happened to me in 2013. I was new to a church however, I was already operating in my purpose, was the CEO of a global magazine, was writing books and hosting conferences and was also a licensed Minister.

Instead of him taking time to get to know me, instead I was directed to join his Minister-in-Training class and asked that I undergo his specific style of leadership in which I agreed. He became my mentor and I paid attention to everything he did. He literally ran the church like a corporation. I leaned and gleaned from him and incorporated a lot of what he did in my own business.

One day I went into his office and shared with him a vision I felt God had given me to start my own business. With him being a business-man I thought he would be the best person to talk to. Boy was I wrong! He shared with me every failed business he and his wife ever had and went on to share how it was no longer about me but about my daughter who was looking up to me. "Your daughter didn't ask to be here," he said. "And she shouldn't have to suffer if this endeavor fails."

I was working in Corporate America at that time and I remember him encouraging me to remain on my job and continue to serve faithfully in the ministry.

I left that day feeling so discouraged. Maybe I didn't hear God, is what I began to think to myself. Maybe he's right. I could never have my own business. What was I thinking to believe that I could do this anyway? These were all the thoughts that began to fill my mind.

I'll never forget during that time I had come across a woman who called herself Real Talk Kim. She and I would keep in touch and talk from time to time after I booked her to speak at my Girl You Rock! Conference in Raleigh, NC.

"You do what God tells you to do. I don't care what your pastor said, and I don't mean no disrespect to him. But your pastor is not God and if that is what God told you to do then you do it and watch the Lord provide," were Kim's words to me.

I hung up the phone feeling activated and as if I could do this. For some strange reason I was no longer afraid. Now please note Real Talk Kim's platform wasn't to the magnitude of where it is today. I believe she was still working at Bloomingdale's and I was the first person to book her to preach (her words, not mine).

She spoke with such authority and it was as if God was using her to tell me, "What did I say?" Perhaps the reason why I second guessed myself was because I already had insecurities and doubts about operating in the marketplace anyway and I was looking for my pastor to validate me and when he didn't my entire world crumbled.

Here's what I learned from this experience: Stop seeking validation from people (this includes your birth and spiritual parents) and receive God's love and acceptance. We all want to be patted on the back and encouraged to pursue our dreams, but we must learn how to encourage ourselves in the Lord just as David (in the Bible) did.

People won't always be there to lift you up and the ones you expect to encourage you to go forward in purpose usually are not the ones to rock out with you.

Have you ever had someone discourage you from what you felt God was prompting you to do? Could it be that God allowed it to train you on how to hear his voice? One of the best things I learned from following Joyce Meyer's ministry since I was a child was, "Sometimes you have to step out to find out." That message still resonates with me today. When I feel Holy Spirit prompting me to do something big and it literally scares me to death, I am reminded that (1) I don't have to do it alone (2) Fear is from the enemy and I belong to God (3) The only time I should be afraid of something is if I am trying to do it without God.

It breaks my heart to know there have been women who ended up involved in adulterous affairs with their pastors or were violated sexually by them. There are too many horror stories of women (and men) being taken advantage of by people who claim to be representing the Gospel of Jesus Christ but are completely mishandling His people.

If you have found yourself currently in a place where you are recovering from a spiritual parent wound(s), I want you to consider this perspective: What lesson is it that God wants you to learn?

One of the things I had to learn was how to honor people of clergy without idolizing them. I wasn't aware that I was doing this, however, when you esteem someone so high to the point you forget they are human, God has a way of reminding you that we are all subject to fall and gifts come without repentance.

I can remember a leader I was once following, and I highly admired her. She was a missionary and could prophesy the paint off the walls. But she would lose her cool during traffic and she gossiped. I remember the first day I was exposed to this type of behavior, I was so disappointed and confused at the same time.

I remember thinking, how does a woman with so much revelation from God lose her cool at another car while driving down the highway. Or how can a woman with so much power and anointing, allow herself to gossip about another church member, while in the presence of other church members?

I'll never forget this time, because my mom and I were in a therapy session and somehow my relationship with this leader came up and our therapist was also a Bishop. He spoke prophetically to me and said, "The Lord is going to show you her humanity because you have placed her up here (while using her hands) when she should only be somewhere in the middle."

My mouth dropped. Huh? I show her too much honor? I remember being so confused until the moment came and I immediately referenced back to his very words.

Simply put, leaders are human, and they make mistakes. There is no perfect leader that exists on the face of this earth. I learned this first hand as I evolved into a leader and people esteemed me to a place where my humanity wouldn't allow me to remain. I made plenty of mistakes and I often reflected on the moment when I judged this leader.

Now, am I trying to excuse what a leader may have done to you? Absolutely not! But what I am trying to do is allow you to step out of your hurt and into the lesson God wants you to learn so that you can grow through what you have been through.

We all have pain and true, none of us deserve some of the hurtful things that have happened to us, however, we can't control it and the best things we can do with situations we can' t control is to place them in the Lord's hands.

There have literally been situations in my life where I didn't understand why God was allowing certain connections to dissolve or some people to respond to me the way they did, but one thing I learned in life is the importance of not taking personal attacks, personally.

Once I learned how to master that, I responded to life with more grace and I stopped getting bent out of shape over every little thing people said or done to me.

Life has taught me in 34 years the importance of going to the throne before going to the phone. Too often people make the mistake of running to another church member to share what their leader did to hurt them instead of praying about it first.

Talk to God about it and tell him how you feel and get into His word. We have become too reliant upon other humans to the point we miss the opportunity to allow God to be God and show up mighty in our lives.

It is my prayer that whatever you are facing right now, that you invite God into that place. Don't try to do life alone. God desires to heal your scars and walk you through your pain.

Remember, prayer is you talking to God, and His Word is how He talks back to you.

HERE ARE THE TOP THREE THINGS HOLY SPIRIT TAUGHT ME WHILE OVERCOMING SPIRITUAL PARENT WOUNDS:

1. **I am ABBA**- Stop looking for a spiritual mama or daddy and focus on your relationship with me. I had it bad. I had mommy and daddy issues therefore, I would cling to spiritual leaders looking for them to validate me and confirm my calling in the earth. We must grow to the place where GOD IS ENOUGH! No more substitutes. I had to learn the hard way that *like* a father is not the same as *being* a father. Even if you were adopted, at times your other "siblings" have a way of reminding you that that's their mommy and/or daddy. The great news is you can have God all to yourself. There is enough of Him to go around!

2. **Wounds Bring Wisdom**- Every life situation we have encountered comes to teach us something. Therefore, we must learn the lesson before we can enjoy the blessing. I know what you have encountered from your leaders was painful and it hurt you to your core and you have vowed to never step foot in another church again (trust me I understand. I've been there and have said those exact same words) but God is saying, "I AM NOT THEM! GIVE ME ANOTHER CHANCE!" There are great people in this world. Not every pastor is a pedophile and not every leader is going to use and

abuse you. However, you must be intentional about keeping God as your central focus and embrace Him as Abba and be careful not to idolize the gift while failing to honor the Gift Giver.

3. **Pain is Necessary for Growth-** It is usually not places of comfort that stretch us to become who we are destined to be. But it is turbulence, painful moments, opposition and our valley experiences that equip us on how to maintain when we transition to the mountain top.

Take a moment and reflect on what has taken place between you and your spiritual leader(s) and identify the lessons you can take away as blessings while surrendering fully to your healing process.

Chapter Nine

Experiencing God as Abba

I'm sure you have heard of the term Abba. It simply means "father."

It took me a long time to grow to the place where I see and believe God to be my Daddy. That's what I call him because that's what I've learned to embrace him as.

The misconception is that our Heavenly Father is so far and completely out of reach when the truth is, he is closer than we could ever imagine.

Have you ever thought about all the blood, sweat and tears you've put into making your marriage or a friendship work? Yet, when it comes to God, we only come to Him when we need Him to fix something.

I used to be that way. I am guilty of at one point in my life, I treated God like he was a Genie in a Bottle. I used to try to bargain with God by saying, "If you do this, I'll do that..." Funny thing was God would always come through, but I'd always fall short in the end.

What this taught me was that I will fail at everything Christ is not at the forefront of (not just the center) but at the beginning, middle and end.

Father's Day was always a holiday I absolutely hated. I used to laugh and say, "Well, that's one holiday I get to save my money on." But it really wasn't funny. I longed to have a relationship with my Dad where I could spend the full day with him. Honestly, I don't recall spending any Father's Day with my dad or buying him a gift.

Although my relationship with my Dad isn't what I desire it to be I still love him however, I had to learn how to embrace God as Abba and allow Him to fill every void, remove every weight and become all I desire.

We don't have the luxury of choosing our families; God does. I used to think he had made a mistake, but then I learned He was intentional about everything he did. The reason I am so passionate about serving others in excellence and treating people properly is because I know what it feels like to be mishandled, pushed aside and cast away.

That's why in my approach to help people I always went after those who had been thrown away by people yet chosen by God. Sure, this came with its own set of battles because when you have experienced a certain level of brokenness and fail to recover, you tend to push away and hurt the very ones that are trying to help you.

I can relate to this because I used to be that person. At one point in my life, I grew so accustomed to people walking away that I would basically dismiss myself before they had a chance to do it. I was standing in my own way and self-sabotage had become my new name.

Years ago, I remember hearing Pastor Sheryl Brady preach a message where she said, "God wants to be whatever you need Him to be, whenever you need Him to be it." That resonated with me so to the point that I wept for what felt like hours.

I often felt so alone and had very few people around me that I felt I could trust. I remember feeling as if I needed God to be so many things to me, but I narrowed it down to, I need God to be my mom and my Dad. For so long I felt both motherless and fatherless and I had completely exhausted myself trying to fix it on my end.

Therefore, I had to back up and fully release it to God and turn it completely over to Him. I learned that He could do more than I could and in a much better way. I would only make a mess.

For so long I felt like an orphan to the point that I felt I had no one, but God and I spent a lot of time being angry with Him because I'm like, God you are the Creator of the Universe. You can do all things! Yet, you had to place me in a situation where I have both mommy and daddy issues?

It was as if I heard the Lord himself say, "I can't nor will I deny another person of their free will." That's when it dawned on me, sometimes we are fighting for a relationship with someone who is not fighting to have one with you. We must grow to the place where we accept what God allows.

Believe it or not, learning to accept this was a vital part of my healing. I had to learn that when someone loves you and desires to be in covenant with you, they will fight for and with you. Sometimes, you must back away and redirect your energy to those who do love and embrace you rather than focusing on those who don't.

I strongly believe God wants to redeem our orphan memories. However, the only way this can happen is if we:

- Recognize the fruit (our emotions)
- Recognize the root (asking God to show us the cause of those emotions or lack of emotions)
- Surrender the event or events and submit them to Jesus
- Repent and forgive those who may have wounded us
- Replace the lie (orphan mentality) with the truth ("Abba Father" relationship) by the renewing of our mind
- Break the stronghold this event(s) has had on our life by allowing God to redeem them and use them

I encourage you not to take your understanding of your Heavenly Father from personal experiences with your birth father. But take it from His word. God is a good, good father and He will never abandon you.

God loves you and He has been waiting to wrap His arms around you however, He's a perfect gentleman and surely wouldn't want to impose. Take a moment, close your eyes, take one deep breath in and one deep breath out (repeat 4X).

Invite God into your space; into your place of hurt, pain, betrayal and emptiness. God specializes in special cases such as yours. Know that you are not alone, and God has not forgotten you. Give Him your whole heart today.

As you conclude this chapter, head over to You Tube and type in: Closer: Wrap Me in Your Arms by William McDowell and allow this song to minister to you.

If you desire to experience God in a way in which you never have, I encourage you to grab your Ipad, computer, or whatever electronic device of choice and go to William McDowell's playlist and let it play through.

Beginning and ending your days in worship is a great way to spend time with Abba. Experiencing his majesty will melt your pain away if you would commit to being consistent and have a genuine desire to know Him in a new way in which you've always desired.

LYRICS

Closer/Wrap Me in Your Arms
William McDowell

Into your arms
I'm drawing near again
To dwell with you
It's my only heart's desire
It's my only heart's desire

And all I can do
Is fall on my knees and cry
Cleanse me with fire
And purify my heart

Draw me close
Closer than before
Closer than I've ever been

Draw me close
Closer than before
Closer than I've ever been

Into your arms
I'm drawing near again
To dwell with you
It's my only heart's desire
It's my only heart's desire

All I can do
Is fall on my knees and cry
Cleanse me with fire
Purify my heart

Draw me
Draw me close
I wanna be, closer than before
Closer than, closer than I've ever been

Oh God, hear the cry of your people

Draw me close
We wanna be
Closer than before
Closer than, closer than I've ever been

Oh God, oh God
Draw me close
Draw me close
Closer than before
I...

Another song I play on repeat is "Give Me You" By Shana Wilson. You can search this song on You Tube as well. Here are the lyrics:

Give Me You
<u>Shana Wilson</u>

Solo: Give me you.
Everything else can wait.
Give me you.
I hope I'm not too late.
Lord, give me you.
Lord, give me you.
Lord, give me you.
Lord, give me you.
(repeat)
It's me oh, Lord.
I'm on my knees.
Crying out to you.
It's me oh; Lord I'm on my knees.
So, give me you.
Give me You.

All: Give me you.
Everything else can wait.
Give me you.
I hope I'm not too late.
Lord, give me you.
Lord, give me you.
Lord, give me you.
Lord, give me you.
(repeat)
Give me you.
Everything else can wait.
Give me you.
I hope I'm not too late. Lord, give me you.)
Lord, give...

HERE IS A LIST OF TWENTY SONGS TO ADD TO YOUR PLAYLIST AS YOU BEGIN YOUR NEW JOURNEY OF EXPERIENCING GOD AS ABBA.

1. We Will Worship – WWW Movement
2. Let Your Power Fall- James Fortune
3. The Call- Isabel Davis
4. Never Be the Same- Shana Wilson
5. For Your Glory- Tasha Cobbs
6. Heart of Worship- Tasha Cobbs
7. Spirit Break Out- William McDowell
8. Victory Belongs to Jesus- Todd Dulaney
9. Just Want You- Travis Greene
10. You Waited- Travis Greene
11. This Altar- Psalmist Raine
12. You Are Welcome- Psalmist Raine
13. Fill Me Up- Casey J
14. Let Your Glory Fill This House- Tonya Baker
15. Miracles- Tonya Baker
16. Yes- Shekinah Glory
17. Nobody Like You Lord- Maranda Curtis
18. You Deserve It- JJ Hairston & Youthful Praise
19. Holy Spirit- Kari Jobe
20. 10,000 Reasons (Bless the Lord)- Matt Redman

Chapter Ten

The Hurt That Healed Me

"Instead, God chose things the world considers foolish in order to shame those who think they are wise. And he chose things that are powerless to shame those who are powerful."
- I Corinthians 1: 27

I never thought I would be writing a book of this caliber and I must admit it was one of the hardest to write. But now, that we are at the end of it I feel such a release and I'm like wow! God, we did it!

Writing a book is symbolic to giving birth to a baby. It can be painful in the process but once you push it out and see how much joy it brings, you forget all about the pain and appreciate your new bundle of joy!

As our time together comes to an end, I want to encourage you to develop a new perspective about all you have gone through and will encounter while here on earth.

What if I told you God allowed hurt into your life to heal a much more deep-rooted issue as well as draw you closer to Him? After many years of studying the life of Jesus and spending time in His presence, I've learned that He will go through extreme measures to ensure we become all we were destined to be despite detours and delays.

I want you to take a moment and repeat this aloud 7X:

THE HURT THAT HEALED ME
THE HURT THAT HEALED ME
THE HURT THAT HEALED ME
THE HURT THAT HEALED ME
THE HURT THAT HEALED ME
THE HURT THAT HEALED ME
THE HURT THAT HEALED ME

Repetition is key when learning new things and I want you to really get this deep down in your spirit that what the enemy intended to hurt you, God desires to use it to catapult you.

Your current hurt whether self-inflicted or caused by another human being, is only there to heal a much deeper issue. We have been treating the symptom far too long, now is the time to get to the root of the matter.

God loves you too much to allow you not to get out of the storm what He intended for it to teach you.

As you shift your perspective, I encourage you to make God a priority in your life. I know it's tough because you can't see him in the natural but with your spiritual eyes sharpened you will begin to recognize Him in all things.

It is my prayer that God will destroy every stronghold that has been attached to your life up until this point. You shall be free in Jesus' name! Forgive! Love! Extend Grace! REPEAT!

God loves you and I declare that you are no longer father-less but you have ABBA as your Daddy!!!! Embrace Him and commit to getting to know Him because there's so much He wants to share with you!

Prayer of Hope

"*Daddy,* I am grateful for your presence and I pray that I abide in you forever. As I conclude this study, help me to retain the information learned and reach back to it as a reference guide. Remind me daily of your love for me. Teach me how to extend love to others the way you have extended it to me. I accept myself as your daughter. I receive your love for me, and I am grateful for who I am becoming in you. Teach me how to use my experiences to help lift others out of the pit of darkness and strengthen them while on their journey. I am so grateful that you love me. I am no longer fatherless, for I call you ABBA!

In Jesus' name, Amen."

Take a moment and write out a personal prayer. Allow the words to flow from your heart and spirit onto the pages. Remember that your Daddy is a tear interpreter and he can read exceptionally well.

_____

_____

_____

_____

_____

_____

_____

_____

_____

_____

_____

_____

_____

_____

_____

_____

_____

_____

_____

_____

Forgiveness Activity

1. Who is it that you carry in your spirit that you need to release that hurt you?

   _____

   _____

   _____

2. What did they do to you?

   _____

   _____

   _____

   _____

   _____

   _____

3. Are you tired of carrying it? If yes, write a letter of release below beginning with....
   Today I release....

   _____

   _____

   _____

_____

_____

_____

_____

_____

_____

4.   Write down how you feel

_____

_____

_____

_____

_____

_____

5.   Who can you share this experience with that can hold you accountable and to ensure you release the offense wholeheartedly?

_____

_____

_____

_____

_____

6. Take a moment and call them.

Did they answer? Did you have to leave a voice mail? If so, send them a text stating it's urgent and that you need to speak with them.

It's important that you not try to go through this process alone. Why do so when you don't have to. More people care about you than you realize.

Silence the voices. Sure, everyone has their own problems but hey you've helped people before, too right? Right.

7. What was the conversation like?

_____

_____

_____

_____

_____

_____

_____

_____

_____

_____

Forgiveness is a process in which we do by faith. Continue to ask Holy Spirit to heal your heart and to teach you how to love like you've never been hurt. I'm so proud of you for making the decision to participate in your own rescue!

How to Detox Your Spirit After Experiencing Heartbreak

(Excerpt from Emotional Detox: 7 Steps to Release Toxicity & Energize Joy by Sherianna Boyle)

During challenging times we have two choices: to sit in reactivity or heal. The journey begins with a decision to heal. Not just the fresh but also the old scars.

1. **DAILY MOVEMENT**: Get Up & Moving. Doing so significantly decreases symptoms of anxiety, making it easier for you to tone down reactivity.

2. **HYDRATE**: Drink plenty of water. When you are dehydrated it can cause symptoms such as headaches, anxiety, fatigue, clogged pores, insomnia and mental confusion.

3. **PROBIOTICS:** A great way to consume healthy bacteria that will help you remove toxins. Mixing one tablespoon of organic apple cider vinegar with a glass of water is an affordable way to do this.

4. **LIMIT DAIRY:** Multiple studies have linked dairy to mood instability and depression. Dairy produces mucus (which contains toxins which if not cleared can cause weight gain.) Almond and coconut milk are great substitutes. Each offer calcium without bloating and gassiness dairy can cause.

5. **MINIMIZE ALCOHOL CONSUMPTION:** They have a way of lowering our level of consciousness so that we are less aware of our bodily sensations. To truly detox your emotions (reactivity), you must have bodily awareness.

6. **CLEAN UP YOUR FOOD:** Select foods that are whole or unprocessed which means they are closest to their most natural (whole and organic) state- foods that are low in sodium, sugar, dyes, and processing.

7. **REDUCE DISTRACTIONS & RESPONSIBILITIES:** During your time of healing it's important that you limit distractions and extra responsibilities. Distractions keep you from receiving the energy, wisdom and strength your emotions can offer. For the

next six months minimize your exposure to distractions.

8. **REQUEST & ACCEPT HELP:** To truly support the emotional atmosphere of your detox, you are going to have to be willing to both ask and accept help. Say yes to receiving support and then reflect upon and ask for what you need. It may be as simple as asking for clarification on something that was said, telling someone you could use a hug, or receiving a gesture of kindness.

9. **SLEEP:** Without a consistent and adequate amount of rest, we run the risk of over processing our emotions. On average, adults need a minimum of seven to eight hours of sleep per day.

- Check out Sherianna's C.L.E.A.N.S.E. Method:

C- lear

L- ook Inward

E- mit

A-ctivate Joy

N- ourish

S- urrender

E-ase

Your Next Step...

I'd love to coach you to success on how to maneuver through life using various resources that have helped (and are still helping) me to not only recover from heartbreak but also how to maintain freedom from anxiety and depression in the process.

If you found this book helpful and are interested in scheduling a Complimentary Strategy Session with me to discuss the next steps to moving forward I'd love to be of service to you.

Simply:

1. Call 888-502-2228 Extension 2 OR
2. Email: carla@womenofstandard.org.
- Be sure to mention you recently read my book & are interested in the complimentary 20 minute Strategy Session I am offering.

Beloved Scriptures

1 Corinthians 15:58

"Therefore, my beloved brethren, be steadfast, immovable, always abounding in the work of the Lord, knowing that your toil is not in vain in the Lord."

James 2:5

"Listen, my beloved brethren: did not God choose the poor of this world to be rich in faith and heirs of the kingdom which He promised to those who love Him?"

Colossians 3:12

"So, as those who have been chosen of God, holy and beloved, put on a heart of compassion, kindness, humility, gentleness and patience."

More Scriptures Centered Around God's Love for You

(Shared from www.crosswalk.com by Kelly Balarie)

You are altogether beautiful, my darling; there is no flaw in you. (Sol. 4:7)

*She is clothed with strength and dignity; she can laugh at the days to come. (**Prov. 31:25**)*

*You will be a crown of splendor in the LORD's hand, a royal diadem in the hand of your God. (**Is. 62:3**)*

*My beloved spoke and said to me, "Arise, my darling, my beautiful one, come with me. (**Song 2:10**)*

*She opens her mouth with wisdom, and the teaching of kindness is on her tongue. (**Prov. 31:26**)*

*Those who look to him are radiant, and their faces shall never be ashamed. (**Ps. 34:5**)*

*You made all the delicate, inner parts of my body and knit me together in my mother's womb. Thank you for making me so wonderfully complex! (**Ps. 139:13-16**)*

Your workmanship is marvelous – how well I know it. (__Psalm 139:13__ – 14)

For we are God's masterpiece... (__Eph. 2:10__)

...Created to do good works which God prepared in advance for us to do. (__Eph. 2:10__)

Blessed is she who has believed that the Lord would fulfill his promises to her! (Lu. 1:45)

God is within her, she will not fall; God will help her at break of day. (__Ps. 46:5__)

And the God of all grace, who called you to his eternal glory in Christ, after you have suffered a little while, will himself restore you and make you strong, firm and steadfast. (__1 Pet. 5:10__)

And who knows but that you have come to your royal position for such a time as this? (__Es. 4:14__)

But you are a chosen generation, a royal priesthood, a holy nation, His own special people, that you may proclaim the praises of Him who called you out of darkness into His marvelous light; (__1 Peter 2:9__)

*For our citizenship is in heaven, from which we also eagerly wait for the Savior, the Lord Jesus Christ. (**Phil. 3:2**0)*

But the Lord said to Samuel, "Do not look on his appearance or on the height of his stature, because I have rejected him. For the Lord sees not as man sees: man looks on the outward appearance, but the Lord looks on the heart. (1 Sam 16:7)

Blessed are the pure in heart, for they shall see God. (Mt. 5:8)

*Now you are the body of Christ and individually members of it. (**1 Cor. 12:27**)*

*You are not your own, for you were bought with a price. (**1 Cor. 6:20**)*

*She is worth far more than rubies. (**Prov. 31:10**)*

*But by the grace of God I am what I am. (**1 Cor. 15:10**)*

*See, I have inscribed you on the palms of My hands... (**Is. 49:16**)*

*I have been **crucified with Christ**; it is no longer I who live, but Christ lives in me; and the life which I* *now live in the flesh I live by **faith** in the Son of God, who loved me and gave Himself for me. (**Gal. 2:20**)*

*And, "I will be a Father to you, and you will be my sons and daughters, says the Lord Almighty." (**2 Cor. 6:18**)*

*For in Christ Jesus you are all sons (and daughters) of God, through faith. (**Gal. 3:26**)*

*...the glorious riches of this mystery, which is Christ in you, the hope of glory. (**Col. 1:27**)*

I have called you friends, for all that I have heard from my Father I have made known to you. (Jo. 15:15)

*Therefore, my dear brothers and sisters, stand firm. Let nothing move you. (**1 Cor. 15:58**)*

But to all who did receive him, who believed in his name, he gave the right to become children of God. (Jo. 1:12)

*For you have died, and your life is hidden with Christ in God. (**Col. 3:3**)*

And to put on the new self, created after the likeness of God in true righteousness and holiness. (Eph. 4:24)

So God created mankind in his own image... (Gen. 1:27)

Affirmations to Declare Daily

"I am God's beloved."

"I echo the heartbeat of God."

"It's so amazing to be loved by Him."

"I am not an orphan!"

"I am on the mind of God!"

"I am valuable!"

"I am beautiful!"

"Jesus is My Daddy & He Loves ME!"

Other Books I Recommend Centered Around Inner Healing

Destroying the Spirit of Rejection

John Eckhardt

Experiencing Father's Embrace

Jack Frost

The Abandonment Recovery Workbook

Susan Anderson

Healing the Soul of a Woman

Joyce Meyer

Peace from Broken Pieces

Iyanla Vanzant

The Orphan Syndome

Dr. Nick Eno

Forgiveness

Iyanla Vanzant

Get Over It! Therapy for Healing the Hard Stuff

Iyanla Vanzant

Uninvited

Lysa Terkeurst

Fervent

Priscilla Shirer

Love Like You've Never Been Hurt

Jentezen Franklin

Websites to Be Empowered Daily

WOMEN OF STANDARD

www.womenofstandard.org

JOYCE MEYER

www.joycemeyer.org

DO YOU DESIRE TO GROW DEEPER IN YOUR RELATIONSHIP WITH GOD? PURCHASE CARLA'S NEWEST DEVOTIONAL STUDY & JOURNEY AT WWW.CARLACANNON.COM!

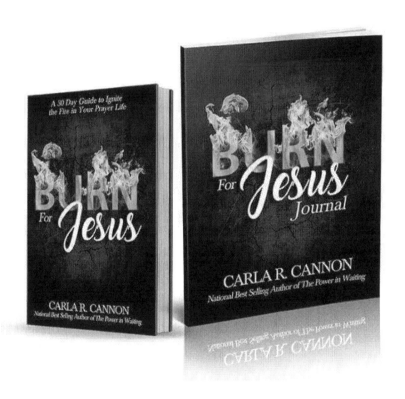

BOOK CARLA TO SPEAK AT YOUR
NEXT EVENT

Speaking Topics:

Although Carla can speak and flow in any atmosphere per your event theme or center focus, here are some of her popular talks that are sure to get your audience unlocked, unleashed & activated!

- **Discover Your T.R.U.T.H**- During this training/conversation, Carla will teach your audience how to (1) **T**ap into Your Testimony (2) **R**est in the Arms of Safety (3) Recognize & Learn to Flow in God's **U**ndying Love for You (4) **T**rain Yourself to Trust & Believe (5) Heal the Hurt of Your Past.

- **Defining the Pearl in You**- During this training Carla will walk your audience through practical steps combined with spiritual truths on how to (1) Unleash the Confident You (2) Get Rid of the Garbage (divorcing the thing(s) that's been hurting you, and (3) Discover Your New Identity.

- **Write Like a Boss**- Carla teaches a 2-hour workshop on how to write a book to launch your business! During this training, Carla will share practical steps on how to (1) Develop Content, (2) Prevent Writer's Block, (3) Organize Your Thoughts (4) Write Your Book in 7 Days and (5) Build a Scalable Business Using Your Book!

Interested?

Send an email to admin@womenofstandard.org with "Booking Inquiry" in the subject line or call: 888-502-2228.

About the Author

Activator, Cultivator, Catalyst & Trailblazer are a few words that describe young mogul in the making, Carla R. Cannon. She is a 9x International best-selling Author & Entrepreneur on a mission to unlock, unleash and activate women into their purpose from the pulpit to the marketplace authentically and un-apologetically with a spirit of excellence.

Carla currently owns and operates **Carla R. Cannon Enterprises, LLC** where she alongside her staff work diligently to equip, empower and educate purpose driven individuals on how to live their dream life without restraints.

Whether it's through live events hosted via her ministry platform, **Women of Standard**, live and virtual trainings through her mentorship program, **Trailblazers Coaching Academy**, Carla (also known to her students as **"Coach C"**) is committed to spreading the love of Jesus in the midst of doing what she calls **"Kingdom Business."**

Carla also prides herself in being what she calls, "God's Mogul" where she teaches emerging and established entrepreneurs from her signature training course: How to Bulletproof Your Business & Bankroll Your Brilliance!

Carla is committed to the advancement of others and is always humbled and honored at any opportunity to share her gift to help others emerge into their life purpose. Whether she has an audience of 1 or 1,000 Carla's energy is magnetic, her presence is radiant, and her heart is filled with the love of **Jesus** ready to share it with all she meets!

Made in the
USA
Columbia, SC